to life

RUTH MINSKY SENDER

to life

RUTH MINSKY SENDER

ALADDIN PAPERBACKS

New York London Toronto Sydney Singapore

First Aladdin Paperbacks edition March 2000

Aladdin Paperbacks
An imprint of Simon & Schuster
Children's Publishing Division
1230 Avenue of the Americas
New York, NY 10020

The Library of Congress has cataloged the
hardcover edition as follows:
Sender, Ruth Minsky. To Life / Ruth Minsky Sender. —1st
ed.   p.   cm.
Summary: A Holocaust survivor recounts her liberation
from a Nazi concentration camp, search for surviving family
members, and long and difficult ordeal of trying to immigrate
with her husband and two children to America.
ISBN 0-02-781831-4 (hc.)
1. Sender, Ruth Minsky—Juvenile literature. 2. Holocaust
survivors—Germany (West)—Biography—Juvenile literature. 3. Refugees, Jewish—Germany (West)—Biography—
Juvenile literature 4. Jews—United States—Biography.]
I. Title.
D804.3.S45 1988   940.53'15'039240-dc
[B]   [92]   88-9312   CIP   AC
ISBN 0-689-83282-6 (pbk.)

To all those who perished
but live in our hearts, a memorial
To all those who found the strength to rise
from the ashes and build a new life, a tribute
To my family, for making life worth living

one

It is February 2, 1950.

"Look, Laibele! Look! The Statue of Liberty!" My voice quivering, my heart singing with joy, I press my little boy's face closer to the porthole of the swaying ship. The long, hard journey, the stormy sea are suddenly forgotten as the shores of freedom reach out to us.

Laibele's eyes glow with excitement as they dance from my face to the tall statue with the torch in her hand. "Is this really America, Mommy? Really?"

I hug him close. The radiant voice of my three-year-old son fills me with bliss. "Yes, Laibele. It really is America. Finally we are here."

My husband, cradling in his arms our seven-month-old son, Avromele, gazes lovingly at us. "Yes, my son, we are finally here." His voice chokes.

I reach out to him, press my face close to his. I feel his warm lips on mine. Tears glide silently from his eyes and mix with mine. "We are free, darling, we are free," I whisper.

"We have a home at last. There is a place for us here. A place for our children."

The happy, excited voices of the refugees surrounding us fade away. My head suddenly fills with sounds of other voices: frightened, dazed, angry voices. My mind wanders back to the barbed-wire cage of the Nazi concentration camp in Germany.

Again it is May 5, 1945. The rising sun slowly chases the shadows of the night, throwing a grayish light on the long rows of rag-clad girls with shaved heads. Our shriveled bodies shiver in the mountain air. Another day of slave labor is beginning. Shovels in hand, we wait for orders to march and dig trenches for the German soldiers.

Around us are the majestic snowcapped mountains of Germany and pretty, picturesque houses. Strange, bony creatures, we clank our wood and canvas shoes against the pebbled roads as we pass the peaceful homes. The cursing of the angry guards, the swishing sound of whips cut through the silence. I wonder if our daily march—the shouts of the guards, the sight of our agonized faces—ever disturbs the people inside those charming homes. What do they think? What do they feel? Do they close their eyes, close their ears, drink their morning coffee, eat their fresh bread, and make believe we are not real?

I, too, sometimes wonder if we are real. Is all this really happening, or is it a horrible nightmare—the barbed wire, the guards, the whips, the slave labor. It must be a nightmare. Soon I will awake at home in my warm bed, Mama bending over me, chasing the nightmare away, saying, *You are safe, you are safe.*

"Are you in another world again?" someone whispers in my ear. "You are marching like a zombie. Something is going on. This road is not the same one we took before."

The fearful words startle me back into painful reality. There is no home. There is no mother, no family. I am all alone here. The nightmare is my daily existence.

The guards curse, swing their clubs over us as they ride along on their bicycles, chasing the marching columns forward. "Faster! Faster, you lazy cows! Do you think you are going for a mountain stroll?"

We drag our wooden shoes, the rough canvas ripping the raw skin of our feet. We run as fast as our worn bodies will move.

Long stretches of woods appear in the distance. Why the woods? My heart beats fast. Maybe they need no more ditches, maybe they have found something new for us to do today. Sometimes they make us carry stones from one place to another and back again. It does not have to make sense to us. We are the slaves. We must follow their orders or be punished. Are they on the run? Are the allies coming close? We hear rumors, whispers.

The end of the war does not mean the end of Germany; it means the end of you! The words repeated so often by the Nazi guards ring menacingly in my ears. *You have nothing to wait for, only the end.* Cold sweat covers my body like a wet blanket.

I think of two days ago. I am knee-deep in mud, digging ditches. Anger, outrage, bitterness fill me. Suddenly I plunge the shovel deep into the mud and stop in silent protest.

The guard above the ditch stares at me. "Are you mad?" His eyes meet mine as he lowers his rifle butt on my head. "You are mad. You are mad."

I hear the girls scream in horror as I slip into the mud. "You *are* crazy, Riva. What did you think you were doing?" One girl wipes my face with her wet, muddy coat. "We are all alone here, Riva, forgotten by the world, at the mercy of murderers. All alone. All alone."

I swallow my tears and dig again. The sound of bombs in the distance brings hope; it brings fear. I clench my teeth. *The bombs do not mean liberation. The day before we die, all of you will die. Remember, you Jewish swine.*

My arms ache. Sweat is pouring over my dirty face as I lift the heavy clay-filled shovel. But then I hear Mama's voice. *As long as there is life, there is hope.* I see her outstretched arms reaching to embrace me. *Hope. Hope. Hope.*

"Riva, do you know what date this is?" Karola, the friend who has been with me through all the horror and pain, from the ghetto through the death camp, Auschwitz, and now in the labor camp, Grafenort, asks sadly.

I stare at her, bewildered. "What difference does the date make? For us each day is the same. Yesterday, today, tomorrow, they do not change. One is as horrifying as the other."

"Riva, it is May third. It is your birthday." A sad smile covers her weary face. "Your birthday, and you are digging ditches." She sighs. "Maybe next year . . . if we survive . . ."

"We must survive, Karola." I raise my voice. "We must hope." I repeat Mama's words eagerly. "As long as there is life, there is hope."

"Work, Jew!" The guard pokes me with his rifle butt. A sarcastic, ruthless grin covers his face. "This is your last birthday, Jew. Next year you will be dead. Next year you all will be dead."

That was two days ago. I still see his cynical grin before me, I still hear his taunting voice. *Next year you all will be dead.*

Frightened whispers buzz all around me. The same horrid thoughts, the same agony fills our minds. The same panic grips our hearts.

The woods are getting closer. My heart beats violently. If we should die here, will anyone remember us? Will anyone survive to bear witness?

I press my notebook, my silent friend, close to me. How many times did the girls in the concentration camp risk their lives to protect these pieces of paper on which I wrote my poems secretly? How many times did they steal paper bags from the garbage in the factory for me, risking punishment if caught? My anger, my sorrow, my hope I poured out on these scraps of paper and shared with the other girls. I hid them all day deep in the sack of straw, my bed, dug them out after a day of hard labor, of carrying buckets of wet clay out of a dark tunnel. My poems, my friends, they helped me hold on to life. Will they be the witnesses of our struggle to live and hope surrounded by horror and death? Will they survive?

I hear girls praying. I join them silently.

The woods spread before us, dark and forbidding, as if warning us not to enter. The first group of girls is already at the edge of the woods. A German guard on a motorcycle speeds by. "Halt! Halt! The Russians are not far behind us!" His agitated outcry rings loud and clear. "Halt! Halt!" The marching columns stop. The guards stop for a moment, then, crazed by the news, take off.

Bewildered, we remain standing on the road. The white houses around us glisten in the morning sun. We are frozen with fear.

"Stand still, girls," someone pleads. "This may be a trick. They may be waiting for us to run, then they will shoot."

We stare at one another, petrified. No one moves.

"Girls, it is not a trick," a girl shouts suddenly, her voice pitched high. "Girls, death was waiting for us in the woods." She sobs, hysterical. "I heard the guards argue. They had orders to kill us. 'We must follow orders!' one said. Then another said, 'Forget about the Jews! Run, save your life!' I heard them. Girls! Girls! We are free! Free!"

Dazed, stunned, we cannot move. The air is heavy with the deadly silence. Suddenly cries break the fear-laden stillness. "They were going to do what they said they would! They were going to murder us! They were going to murder us!"

Tears flow slowly over my sunken cheeks. Mama was right. As long as there is life, there is hope.

I turn my eyes away from the dark, menacing woods. I am still alive. I am free. But where do I go? To whom do I go? In back of me are the woods that were to be my grave. In front of me, roads that lead back to the cage. Where do I go?

"Where do we go?" Others echo my thoughts.

"Let's knock at the doors of those pretty, quiet homes."

"Maybe they will help now, with no guards here."

"Maybe, maybe now they will help."

The white, cozy-looking homes stare silently at us. Frightened, we walk slowly toward them. We knock. Softly at first, then harder and harder. We are pounding with our bony fists against the wooden doors. No one answers.

"There are people inside. I heard them."

"They are hiding from us. There is no one here to help us, to give us shelter, food."

"All the doors are closed to us."

Slowly we drag our frail bodies back, back to the barbed-wire cage of the concentration camp that held us prisoner. The gates stand wide open. No guards are at the watchtower. No guards at the gates. We are dazed, lost. There is no other place for us to go. We are all alone, far from home. Is there a home left? How do we get there? We have no transportation. Should we wait for the Russian liberators? Are we safe? So many questions.

Then we hear shouts and screams coming from a barrack. Some girls drag out a

German guard. He was hiding under a bed of straw. "Please, girls, please. Please do not hand me over to the Russians. They will kill me." He falls to his knees, crying, pleading. "I only followed orders, I only followed orders. Please, please, save me, please. I am not guilty. I only followed orders."

The shouting, the screaming suddenly stop. We stare at one another. Without his rifle, without his whip he is a pathetic, miserable creature. We are his victims. We are his jury. We are his judges. His life is in our hands now.

"Girls, let God be his judge." A voice void of emotion cuts through the silence.

"Let God be his judge," one of the girls repeats slowly. She turns, walks away. Others follow. The guard slowly gets up, moves fearfully past us, then runs through the open gate to his freedom. I watch him disappear.

Numb, weak, we lie again on the sacks of straw. The gates are open, but no one leaves. If our liberators come we will be here, waiting for them.

May 7, 1945. He enters the gates of the cage like a prince in a fairy tale, a Russian officer on a white horse. A small group of tired, muddy soldiers follows slowly. We run toward them. They stare at us as if seeing ghosts rising from the grave. The officer, a middle-aged man, dazed, slowly gets off his horse.

Bony hands reach out to touch him. Is he real?

He stares at us. His voice quivers. He speaks Yiddish. "Are there Jews here?"

"Yes! Yes! We are Jews! We are still alive!"

Tears flow freely over his weatherbeaten face. "You are the first Jews we have found still alive." His voice breaks. "We liberated several concentration camps and found only ashes, dead bodies. I am a Jew. I had given up hope of finding any of my people alive. You are the first . . . the first. . . ."

We are all sobbing. "What happened to our families? Did they—"

He shakes his head sadly. "So many . . . so many . . . so many murdered . . . Thank God I have found some of my people alive." He covers his face with his hands, and a wretched, woeful cry rips through the air.

two

OUR LIBERATORS REST for a few hours, then continue forward to capture the German army on the run. Before they leave they speak of horrors they have seen—of the death and desolation the Nazis have inflicted.

"So many death camps."

"Piles upon piles of dead bodies."

"Mountains of hair, eyeglasses, shoes. Many, many shoes of men, women, children."

"We will never forget the sight, the stench of burned bodies."

"How can we forget? . . . How can we forget? . . ."

Their voices lower to a painful whisper. We cry. They cry. We ask questions. Endless questions. We fear the answers.

"Will we find anyone in our families—alive or dead?"

"How do we search for survivors?"

"How do we get away from here?"

"Where do we go?"

They listen, heads bowed. Their hearts go out to us. They give us food, speak softly, gently.

"Dear girls. Poor girls. You must hold on to hope."

"It will take time to heal your wounds."

"It will take time to search for family, for survivors."

"You must rebuild."

"You must live."

"We must move on. Other Russian soldiers will soon come. They will help you."

"It is sad to leave you here in this horrible place, but you are safe."

I do not feel safe. The barbed wire surrounding us, the guard posts, even empty, still fill me with panic. The gates are open, but it is the same cage. The horrors we saw, the pain, the degradation we endured are still around us. How can I feel safe here?

I turn to my friend. "Karola, let's not stay here any longer. We are free. We cannot wait here for Russian help. It may be months before they take us back to Poland. There is no transportation now. But we are free to go." The agitated words race off my lips. "Karola, maybe someone is still alive. Maybe they are searching for us in Poland, in Lodz. Maybe we will find family." I catch my breath. "It is a very long journey from Germany to Poland on foot, but I have an idea. We will join the Russian slave laborers on their way home to Russia."

She stares at me as if I have lost my mind. "Riva, what are you talking about?

Why should we want to go to Russia? We are from Lodz, Poland, remember?"

"Karola, I am not crazy. Listen." I take her hands in mine. "My sisters, Mala and Chana, and my brother Yankl are somewhere in Russia. They escaped to Russia when the Nazis conquered Poland in 1939. I do not know where to search for them in Russia, it is such a huge country. . . . " I swallow hard. "But we'll search for them. They must be alive. We'll find them. We will find them and together we will all search for the others in my family, in your family."

Karola studies my flushed face. "Riva, maybe . . . maybe they all survived." Her voice is high-pitched, her dark eyes flash with hope as she presses my hand tightly. "Maybe they all survived, my brother Berl, your brothers Motele and Moishele. We survived. They were all young." Her voice breaks. "Last time we saw them was August 27, 1944. We were herded from the cattle cars into the death camp, Auschwitz. They went to one side, we to the other." A painful moan tears from her lips. "We survived, why not they?" She trembles. "I will come with you, Riva. I cannot remain here any longer. You are my only friend, my family. We will go together by way of Russia to Poland."

I gaze around me. Haggard, emaciated girls sit or lie on sacks of straw. "Girls." My voice quivers. "Girls, Karola and I are leaving. Who wants to leave with us?"

Frightened, bewildered, they stare at me. Voices echo throughout the barrack.

"I am too numb to move."

"I am too weak to move."

"I want to wait for transportation."

"I will not move until the Russian army comes."

"We have no one to help us on the outside."

"I am afraid of what we will find outside."

I raise my voice above the others. "Girls, we are free. Remember, we are free to walk out of here now. I will not remain any longer."

Hela, tall, all bones, a kerchief tied around her shaved head, walks toward me. She is in her thirties, one of the very few that old. She often acts like a mother toward us. She folds her bony arms, her eyes fixed on me. "My sister Bela and I will come with you." Her eyes move slowly, gently, over her sister's terrified face. "It will be all right, Bela." Her voice is soft. She turns her gaze toward me again. "I heard you speak to Karola of Russia. We, too, have family that fled the Nazis from Lodz to Russia." Her voice trails off. "Such a large family. Someone, someone must have survived."

Bela nods in silent agreement.

The four of us walk toward the gate. My

heart pounds like a drum, faster and faster. We approach the gate. The pounding within me becomes stronger. We move forward slowly, cautiously. Suddenly I run through the open gate. I am free! I am free! I am free!

The roads are deserted. The Germans are hiding from the Russians. Like hunted prey afraid of a trap, I look around carefully.

With guarded steps we move forward in the gutter. Suddenly Hela stops. Her eyes glow with an angry fire. "Why do we still walk in the gutter like animals? We are human beings again. We are free to walk on the sidewalk. No more walking in the gutter." She marches quickly onto the sidewalk. Our eyes searching for hidden danger, we follow her.

Jews are forbidden on the sidewalk! Off the sidewalk, Jews! echoes in my head. It was 1939 when I heard those shouts as I was kicked off the sidewalk by a German soldier. I was still a child. I still had a family. I still had a home. That was a lifetime ago, many lifetimes ago.

Now I am alone. No family. No home. Now I walk on a sidewalk in a German town where there is not a German in sight. No one to kick me with his heavy boot. No one to hit me with his rifle butt. I walk on a sidewalk in Germany, free. But I feel no joy, no sense of victory.

What road should we take? Where do we turn? Should we knock at a door, ask for food, shelter? Will they let us in? Will they help us? I read the same questions in the eyes of my friends.

"We have no choice, girls." Hela looks from one to the other. "We must knock at their doors."

She walks slowly toward a cozy-looking house. Flowerpots line the window. We follow her with slow, faltering steps, then stop. I feel like an intruder.

Hela knocks softly at the white door. No answer. She knocks again, harder. No answer. She puts her ear to the door. "I hear voices inside," Hela says. She knocks again and again. "Please open up. We want only food. Please, help us."

Not a sound is heard from the house. We sit, weary, hungry, lost, on the front steps. "I know I heard whispering inside," Hela says bitterly. There is a sudden change in her voice. "Well, now they, too, know fear."

We try another house. No answer. "We must find shelter from the cold. It gets very cold at night in the mountains." Bela huddles closer to her sister.

Hela puts her arm around her. "We will be all right, my dear sister. We will be all right."

Night is approaching. We move from house to house, knock, call, plead. "We mean you no harm. We are only girls,

Jewish girls freed from the concentration camp. We want only shelter for the night. Please, help us." But the inhabitants in the warm homes remain silent.

One of the houses has a small barn. Slowly we push the door. It opens with a groan. We jump back, startled. Hela pokes her head carefully through the door. "It looks empty," she whispers. "I see only hay on the ground."

We walk in with hesitant steps, our eyes searching, searching. Assured that we are alone in the barn, each of us falls wearily into the soft hay on the ground. "We have a roof over our heads." Karola sighs. "A barn, but still it is a roof over our heads."

three

I LIE CURLED up in the hay. Thoughts race through my mind, making me shiver. What if we are going in the wrong direction to find the camp of the Russian slave laborers? What if they will not allow us to go home with them? We are not Russians. Sometimes we passed them on our way to work. They cursed the Germans, threw us words of encouragement, even food. It felt good to hear their warm greetings. But will they accept us as traveling companions? If I get to Russia, will I find my sisters and brother there? Russia is so big. Where do I begin to search for them? I have no address. I have not heard from them since 1940.

I remember their last letter, which arrived in the ghetto of Lodz. They were on the way to meet Uncle David, my father's brother who left Poland before I was born. He settled near the Russian city of Kharkov. I remember seeing pictures of him, his wife, and child. Mala wrote: "It is hard to travel from place to place. We need permission. Now the papers we have waited so long for are here, finally. We are eager to be reunited with our uncle. We won't be alone here anymore."

But then Germany attacked Russia. Kharkov was one of the first cities hit. Did they survive the attack?

I think of my father's family in Russia, in Argentina. They all left Poland. They saw no future there. My family remained. Mama would not part with her parents, brothers, sister. *Families should stay together.* Mama's words ring in my ears.

My head spins. I press my eyes tightly together. We tried so hard to stay together. . . . What will I tell Mala, Chana, Yankl when I find them? We tried. We tried to stay together, but . . .

Where is Mama? I bite my lips. On September 10, 1942, the Nazis surrounded the ghetto and took her from us. Did she survive? Did she have the strength to go on living, torn from her children? Did she hold on to hope? *As long as there is life, there is hope.* Her words stayed with me each time I wanted to give up. Did *she* give up?

What do I tell Mala, Chana, and Yankl about our younger brothers, Motele, Laibele, Moishele? Tears glide over my face and disappear into the soft hay around me. I see Laibele's pale, gentle face before me. He held on to life as long as he could. He died in my arms on April 23, 1943. He was only thirteen years old. My body swollen from malnutrition, my legs useless from the loss of calcium, I watched in horror as the burial squad placed the body of my dear little brother on a wagon piled high with the other dead and rushed them off to the cemetery for burial. But at least I know that in the Jewish cemetery in Lodz he has a grave. . . .

Where are the others? Did Motele and Moishele survive Auschwitz? I survived. They were always the stronger ones, always worried about my health, my strength. I faced death many times, yet survived. Where are they? I hear Motele's voice again, pleading with our friend as we sit crammed together in the dark, hot, smelly cattle car. *Please, take care of my sister. She always had us to watch over her. Please, she is not very strong. They may separate us. Please, look after her.*

I hear the shout of the Nazi guards as the cattle cars are opened. *Welcome to Auschwitz, Jews! Men to the right! Women to the left! Fast! Fast!* I hear my horrified scream. *Motele! Moishele! Do not leave me alone!*

"Motele, Moishele, do not leave me alone," I whisper, bringing the hay closer to my shivering body. I must still hope. . . . I survived. . . .

When I find them, I must tell my sisters and brother of the letters I wrote to them, knowing very well there was no mail going out of the ghetto. Still, I wrote. I wanted them to know of our struggle, our hopes, our daily fight for life, for dignity. When they came back, I reasoned, they would read the letters. And if we should not survive, the letters would bear witness to our spiritual resistance. I carried those letters to Auschwitz with poems I had written. They remained there with all our other possessions. Maybe they are mingled together with the ashes of those who perished in Auschwitz.

What if I don't find anyone?

The sound of voices from outside the barn startles us. We huddle together, listen, afraid to move. "They speak Russian." Karola jumps up. "Our liberators are here." We run to the barn door, open it quickly, and step back. We are face-to-face with several Russian soldiers pointing their rifles at us. They stare wildly at our horrified faces. Our sunken cheeks, ashen faces, short crop of hair, and bony skeletons wrapped in rags tell where we came from. They lower their rifles.

"Jewish girls?"

"What are you doing here?"

"Why are you hiding in a barn?"

"You could have been shot by us."

"Poor girls, you are shivering."

"Do you have blankets?"

"Do you have food?"

They all speak at once. Their voices are filled with compassion, with outrage.

"Why aren't you in one of the warm homes?" one shouts, pointing his rifle at the homes around us.

"They will not let us in," we reply.

He turns quickly toward the door, calls to another soldier. "Come, comrade, we will find a place for these girls." The two of them hurry out of the barn.

The sound of banging at a door, then the cracking of wood, voices. The two Russian soldiers return, pushing before them a middle-aged woman and an old man. Fear is written on their faces as they are pushed toward the hay on the ground. They beg for mercy. "We do not know anything. We did not do anything."

"Look at these girls," one of the Russians shouts in German. "Look! Look at them! Beg them for mercy! Look what the Germans did to them! Look! Look!" He pushes them toward us. "Look! Look! Why did you not let them in, give them shelter, give them food, you Nazi beasts. I should kill you right here!"

"We did not know anything. We did not know anything," mumbles the old man meekly.

"We are not guilty," the woman wails.

"Yes! You are guilty! You are all guilty! You are guilty for keeping silent!" a Russian shouts. He shoves them toward the pile of hay. "You stay here! Girls, come into the house."

"Thank you, thank you," the man mumbles as they crawl into a corner of the barn. "Thank you, thank you."

four

WE ENTER A warm, charming kitchen. The embroidered white curtains hang neatly pressed on the windows lined with flower-pots. Colorful knickknacks glow on shelves on the kitchen walls. A secure, comfortable, orderly nest where they shared their hardy meals, while we, driven like animals, passed daily under their windows. But they did not see, they did not hear, they did not know. . . . *You heard! You saw! You kept silent! You are guilty!* something within me shouts.

Within minutes the table is laden with bread, butter, cheese, milk. We stare at the food as if it were a dream that might vanish. "Eat, girls, eat." A sandy-haired soldier with warm blue eyes smiles at us. "Do not be afraid. Eat. Eat."

Slowly we move toward the table and then hungrily, eagerly shovel large chunks of food into our mouths. How many years have we dreamed of this? A table laden with food. Bread, bread, bread, as much as we can eat.

The soldiers drink beer as they watch us devour the food. There are five of them, all young, serious.

"Where are you girls planning to go on foot, alone?" one asks after a while. His voice is low and sad. "What country are you from?"

The girls look at me. My heart beats faster. My voice quivers. "We are from Poland and are trying to get to Russia."

"Why Russia?"

I swallow the lump in my throat. "My sisters and brother are in Russia."

He looks puzzled. "In Russia? How did they get to Russia?"

"In 1939 they fled to Russia to escape the Nazis." I take a deep breath. "For a short time we received mail and packages of food from them. Then the Nazis herded the Jews into a ghetto and all mail stopped." I continue nervously. "We have an uncle in Russia, near Kharkov. My sisters and brother wrote in their last letter that they were trying to get to Kharkov. I don't know if they got there. I don't know where they are. But I must find them." My voice sounds strange. My face feels hot and moist.

The Russian puts his arm around my shoulder. "Russia, too, suffered from the Nazis. Kharkov, the big, beautiful city, was attacked by them. Many cities were destroyed. Millions of civilians, millions of soldiers died." He sighs deeply. "Russia is a big country. Many places are destroyed, in chaos. You may not be able to find your family." He takes my hand in his.

I feel wretched, hopeless. Tears glide down my cheeks. He wipes them with his sleeve. "Poor girl. It is sad, but true."

"How did you plan on getting to Russia?" a tall, slim soldier asks.

"We hoped to join the Russians returning home from slave labor in Germany. They must have a way of getting home." My voice cracks.

"No, they do not." There is anger in his voice. "They do not. There are so many of them, and so few trains to bring them home. You must remember, girls, you are not Russians. You are from Poland. You must go back to Poland."

I stare at my friends helplessly. They, too, look beaten.

The young, buoyant voice of one of the soldiers breaks the painful stillness. His eyes twinkle with an inner glow. "Girls, you are alive. You are free. You survived Hitler. Do not give up. You will make it home." He turns to one of his comrades. "Hey, Boris, play your harmonica for us. These poor girls need cheering up. Play us a pretty Russian tune."

Boris, a warm smile on his round, ruddy

face, takes a small harmonica from his coat pocket. Playfully he tosses his light brown hair away from his eyes. He puts the harmonica to his lips. Enchanting, soft music fills the room. The sound of the beautiful music, the warm, friendly faces around us bring tears to my eyes. I gaze at my friends. They, too, are crying.

Boris stops playing, stares confused from one to the other. "I do not want you to be sad, girls. No tears. No tears."

He starts another tune, bouncy, gay. His comrades clap their hands joyfully to the beat of his music. "Come, girls, clap your hands," they urge us.

It feels so strange, so unreal. Sitting in a warm kitchen, not feeling any hunger, surrounded by smiling faces, clapping hands to music. Could it be that only this morning we were surrounded by the barbed-wire cage of the concentration camp? "Hey, girl, stop dreaming. Let's dance." The sandy-haired soldier pulls me off the chair playfully. I stiffen. He pulls me closer. I pull back.

"Let her be, comrade. She is frightened and weak," Boris intervenes.

The soldier holding my arm looks annoyed at his comrade and lets go of my arm. I sit down. My heart beats fast. He, too, sits down. He rests his elbows on the table and cradles his head in his hands. His eyes move from one girl to the other. There is a strange glow in them. "Well." His voice is loud and menacing. "Well, are you girls too frightened, too weak to go to bed with us, too?" He gets up from the table angrily. "Well, girls, will you come or will I have to force you?"

There is a choking stillness in the room. I gasp for air. We look horrified at one another. Hela's petrified eyes meet mine. She takes a deep breath. "Comrade, we were lucky." Her shaking voice betrays her fear. "We survived the Nazi hell." She looks straight at him now. "You are our liberators. Surely you do not want to harm us. You would not force us to do something against our will. You are too kind to bring us more pain."

There is deadly silence. I sit frozen in the chair, but my eyes move pleadingly from one soldier to the other. *Do not bring us more pain.*

"You ungrateful Jewish dogs." The sandy-haired soldier curses. "You are too scared to show your appreciation to your liberators. I should teach you a lesson, you Jewish cowards!"

Cold sweat covers my body. I hear a silent scream within me.

"Leave them alone, comrade." The soldier with the sad, gentle voice puts his arm around his furious friend. "They've suffered enough." He turns to the others. "We should put on patrol, comrades." He leaves. The others follow.

We bolt the door quickly. Holding on to one another, we cry.

five

ALL DAY LONG we march. The German villages and towns look empty and deserted. I wonder where the Germans are hiding. We come across some old German men. They are afraid of us. "We did not know what was going on," they repeat pathetically. "We are not guilty." I stare at them as they try hard to convince us of their ignorance, their innocence. I want to shout, *Murderers!* But they look so pitiful, deplorable. I walk off without saying anything.

We meet other survivors. They have come from the many concentration camps that were spread over Germany. The horror stories of death camps, gas chambers, labor camps lessen the hope of finding family alive.

It has been three weeks since our liberation from the barbed-wire cage of the concentration camp. We hug and kiss each survivor we come across. We are one another's family now. We exchange names, former home addresses, places of destination.

The questions are always the same.

"Where are you from?"

"Were you in the camps, hiding? Or were you with the partisans?"

"Where are you heading?"

"Did you ever hear my name in the camps?"

The answers are also the same.

"No, no. We did not know last names."

"We had to remember our numbers. We were only numbers."

The pleas, too, are the same.

"Remember my name. Maybe someone will ask for me."

"Remember, I am from Poland— Krakow, Lodz, Warsaw."

"Remember, I am from Budapest, Hungary."

Many names of countries, cities, towns, some of which I have never heard before, spin in my head. "Remember. Remember. Remember."

The more we hear, the less hope we have. We speak of our fears in low, subdued voices, as if a terrible secret that lurks for us in the shadows might attack, consume us with its ugliness and horror if we raise our voices above a whisper.

"We must hope."

"We must not give up."

We find shelter for the night in an empty barn. The four of us huddle together for warmth and strength.

"Girls, we held on to life for six years. Through the ghetto, the slave labor and death camps. We held on to hope. We must not give up now." Hela wipes the tears off her sister's face. "We must hope that someone, somewhere, did survive. We must hope. . . ."

We cry ourselves to sleep.

Searching for food and shelter in empty homes and barns, hiding from Germans, hiding from Russians, our bony shadows move slowly through the ghost towns of Germany. I must reach Poland. Someone may be waiting for me there. My feet move faster, pushed by an invisible force.

We reach the Polish border. We have been marching for three weeks to reach this point. It is still a very long way from Lodz. The train station is swarming with people dressed in rags, searching with tormented eyes the faces of strangers.

"Did you hear . . ."

"Did you see . . ."

"My name is . . ."

Names. Names. Addresses. The air is ringing with names, addresses. Strangers pass slips of paper from hand to hand. If someone should ask, remember. . . . Remember. . . . Remember. . . .

six

LODZ. HOW STRANGE it feels to walk in its streets again. A lifetime has passed, but the streets have remained the same. Even the people moving in and out of the buildings have not changed. Only we have changed, the Jews of the city of Lodz; we are not the same as before. We are the ghostly remnants of what was a lively, creative, sparkling Jewish community, now wandering, searching the streets of the city we once knew, for traces of family, of friends.

Karola, Hela, Bela, and I make our way out to the area that was the ghetto of Lodz. *Move quickly, move quickly,* voices in my head shout. *Maybe someone is waiting for you.* But my legs drag heavily, afraid to enter. The barbed wire is gone. The guard posts are gone. Again this area is part of the city of Lodz. A part that speaks of horror, of struggle, of hope, of people who are no more. Some of the homes are empty. Broken glass, broken furniture, torn pictures, pieces of lives lie scattered in the rubble.

Karola and I walk slowly toward the

street where we both lived in the ghetto, Berka-Joselewicza. I gaze at Hela and Bela as they turn in the direction of their former home. home. They walk tentatively, silently. I hope that we will meet again someday.

Berka-Joselewicza 18. I stare at the building. This was the home I shared with my brothers Motele and Moishele. My heart pounds faster and faster. Will they be there? Will they come to the door to welcome me home? Do I hear them calling me?

My heart stops. A Polish woman stands in the doorway of our apartment. She stares at me with anger and suspicion. "What are you looking for? What do you want?"

"I have come back from the camps," I stammer. "I lived here for years."

Through the partially open door, our furniture stares back at me. *Why did you come back alone? You did not leave alone. . . .* I feel guilty that I have come back. I feel guilty that I have survived.

The woman, strong and healthy-looking, keeps her eyes glued to my face. Her eyes also ask, *Why did you survive? Why did you come back? Who needs you here?* She blocks the doorway. "This is my home now," she shouts. "The Jewish homes were given to us Poles. What do you want here?"

"I do not want anything." My voice is hollow, strange. "I came to search for my family. Did anyone ask for me?" I stare at her. She lowers her eyes.

"No. No." She does not move away from the doorway.

"Please, let me look for pictures of my family. I want only pictures. I want to remember them, please."

"I have no pictures," she says loudly. "I threw them out with the books I found here."

I feel a sharp pain in my heart. The books. Three hundred books. Motele's excited face flashes before my eyes. I heard his voice again. *The secret library will be perfect in this corner. We have a back door, easy for people to come and go from without attracting attention. We'll put up curtains over the shelves, and it will look like a closet. Riva, Moishele, let's do it. Let's bring the secret library to this house.*

The books we risked our lives for survived, and she threw them into the garbage. The witnesses of our struggle for dignity— she threw them into the garbage.

"What did you do with the garbage? Where did you throw it?"

The sound of my voice scares her. She steps back as if I were going crazy and might attack her.

"It was in the backyard, but some people came—some of *your* people—to search for the books. All they wanted were the books."

I run to the backyard. Torn books,

broken glass, broken pieces of furniture, traces of my life, my family are scattered over the yard. But no pictures. No pictures.

I take a last look at the place that once was my home. The place I shared with the people I loved. The place where together we hoped, studied, held on to life, helped one another survive, dreamed of a new tomorrow.

Now this is tomorrow. And I am a lone survivor searching in the garbage for traces of my family. I hold on to the walls of the building, crying bitterly. Then I leave, my heart overflowing with pain and anger.

I drag myself to the Jewish cemetery of Lodz. I find Laibele's grave all covered with weeds. I clean them away gently, as if I were cleaning again my dear little brother. I sit on the ground and talk to him as I used to when he lay in his bed, dying from tuberculosis and listening to my tales of tomorrow.

"I am here with you again, little brother. Why did I come back and not Motele, not Moishele? Now I, too, must leave. I cannot live here. This earth is soaked with our blood."

I sit and stare at the bare grave. "I will make you a tombstone to keep the weeds from covering your marker: Laibele Minski. Died April 1943, age 13. In the ghetto of Lodz."

I search for a brick in the rubble. I find the white metal headboard of a child's bed. I drag it away from the pile of junk and put it at the head of the grave. "That is your tombstone, little brother," I whisper hoarsely.

I sit for hours and cry. I cry for his lost young life. I cry for all those who do not have any graves, any traces. I cry for the lonely survivors who must go on.

I leave to meet Karola. Her ashen face and red, swollen eyes speak for her. No sign of her family.

Silently we embrace and cry. "Karola, we must not come back to this place anymore." I take her hand in mine. Together we walk off to search for survivors.

seven

THE JEWISH COMMITTEE for the Relief of Jews Returning to Lodz is filled with people. Newly formed by the first survivors to return, the committee is hard at work trying to reunite families. Lists of known survivors are posted on the walls, which are also covered by the messages of some who passed through here and went on to search in other places. Eagerly we look quickly over the lists, searching for familiar names. Once in a while we hear an outcry of joy. "I found a brother." "I found a sister." "I found a friend." The happiness of the lucky survivor becomes everyone's for the moment. Then the pain returns.

Some cry quietly. Others ask questions that have no answers. "Why can't I find somebody? Why must I remain alone?" wails a middle-aged woman. "God in heaven, why? Where are my children?" My heart breaks as I listen to her. I think of Mama and wonder how many times she asked the same painful question. Where is she now?

I move to the lines at the registration

desk. We have to register so that our names can appear on the lists of survivors. The lines move very slowly. My heart pounds. Maybe when I give my name they will know of someone searching for me. Maybe I will find someone. Maybe . . . But I find no one. Karola finds no one, either. Dejected, we move on.

I hear people's voices as I pass the lines of survivors hoping for miracles.

"Better luck next time."

"Do not despair, friends. Our people are just beginning to return."

"Do not lose hope."

At night we lie on the floor of a huge building that shelters survivors. We have no homes to return to. We listen to one another's horror stories, repeated again and again, hang on to one another's words. Maybe we will hear a name, a familiar name, maybe some sudden news, some clue to where they all vanished.

"The Jews of the Lodz ghetto taken during the Nazi raids in 1942 were gassed in trucks in Chelmno. The trucks had Red Cross emblems. The people did not know what was waiting for them inside. Death. Death was waiting—"

My head spins. I jump up. A horrified scream rips my body. "No! No! My mother was taken during those raids. She has to be alive!"

Someone caresses my head as I squirm

on the hard floor. Mama! Mama! From the open window come sounds of a bird singing happily. Rays of sunshine play on the faces of the shriveled bodies on the cold floor. I stare at the window with swollen red eyes and ask, Why? Why? Why?

Each day we search the lists with eager eyes, with pounding hearts. We look at faces in the street, listen for familiar voices. I run after a woman whose walk seems familiar. I grab her hand. She turns around, stares at me. "You damned Jews! You're back again." My knees buckle under me, sweat covers my body as I watch her walk away with quick, angry steps.

I hold on to Karola's arm. "There is nothing here for us anymore, Karola. We left our names with the Jewish Committee. There is nothing else. . . ." A painful sigh heaves my chest. "I heard that the Polish Jews who escaped the Nazis to Russia have been allowed to return to Poland. They say that those transports come to Wroclaw."

Karola's eyes are on my face.

"Karola, let's go to Wroclaw. My sisters, Mala and Chana, my brother Yankl may be among them. Please, come with me."

She puts her arm around me. "Riva, I would not let you wander so far all alone. I will go with you, but let's ask Oscar to join us." She blushes suddenly. "I like him. I think he likes me, too." Her cheeks are bright red now. "It will be safer to have a man with us. With all the Russian soldiers around here, it will be safer. It is a very long journey from Lodz to Wroclaw, Riva."

Oscar is happy to come with us. "I cannot let you two lost souls wander alone all over Poland." He smiles, embracing both of us protectively.

We change trains several times. The trains are filled with people wandering all over Poland, searching for traces of family. Maybe, maybe in Wroclaw I'll find my family.

Wroclaw, formerly the German city of Breslau, is now part of Poland. Piles of rubble, empty shells of bombed buildings line the streets. We wander among the ruins, looking for shelter in the homes that remain intact. One apartment that we enter still has dirty dishes in the sink. The plumbing is damaged. The only water supply is an old pump in the yard. We are joined by other survivors as we explore the empty building. Scattered papers, books, clothing, valuables tell of a hurried escape.

We will stay here until we find a better place. We begin to clean up. One of the rooms has a huge pile of clothing scattered on the floor. We start to clear it and stop, dazed. Under the pile of clothing lie large sums of German marks. We stare in amazement at the mountain of worthless German money. Someone begins to kick the money frantically. We all join in. We open the window wide and throw the worthless money into the gutter. Shouts of joy fill the room.

"Hitler and his murderers are dead!"

"Germany is defeated!"

"We survived them!"

"We live! We live!"

The door to the apartment is always open. Survivors of death camps, survivors of hiding places, former partisans come and go. They ask questions, leave names, go on to search further for family, friends. Food is hard to come by. A jar of honey found in an empty apartment becomes a meal we all share. Each new survivor we meet is a long-lost friend, not a stranger. We have a common bond: We survived. We are the remnants of our people.

We spend long hours speaking about home, family, childhood. About the ghettos, death camps, labor camps, we speak less and less. The wounds are too raw. We must let them heal. We must go on.

New friendships, new romances blossom. Karola and Oscar are serious about each other. I am so happy watching them exchange loving glances. We rose from the ashes. Life is beginning anew. Our hearts can still feel love. Our faces can still form a smile. Our mouths can still utter words of affection. We are alive. . . .

New people come to Wroclaw daily

with the hope of finding family among the returnees from Russia. Each time we hear that a transport is to stop at Wroclaw, I sit at the train station and wait, hope. Many times the transports come days later than scheduled. Others, too, wait and hope.

When a transport does arrive, the returnees are immediately surrounded. Questions. Questions. Questions.

"Did you hear this name?"

"Did you meet someone who resembles me?"

I study their faces, listen to their voices, hoping, hoping. No one has met my sisters, my brother. I sit at the train station, absorbed in painful thoughts. Suddenly I hear a cry of joy. A familiar voice. "Riva! My dear friend. We are both alive to meet again! Miracles still happen, Riva! My dear friend Riva."

We throw our arms around each other. "Tola! Tola! You helped me survive. You shared your food with me, took care of me."

We hold each other tightly, crying tears of joy. Tola, my friend who took me into her heart in Auschwitz and in the labor camps, is at my side again. She, too, is searching for a brother who escaped to Russia.

"Miracles still happen, Riva." She wipes the tears from her face. "We must believe in miracles."

The transports from Russia, exhausted

from weeks in crowded trains, tell of hunger, suffering, sorrow. They ask many questions. They listen, bewildered, horrified.

"It cannot be. It cannot be. I must go home. I must find my family," a man near me whispers hoarsely, walking back and forth, back and forth. "We must keep on searching. We must hope."

I stare at his tall, skinny figure. His worn coat. He looks as if he has wandered the world. He is searching and will go on searching for a home, a family, a place to rest. "We must hope. We must hope." His voice is low.

Tears flow over my face. "As long as there is life, there is hope," I whisper.

eight

OUR PLUMBING IS still not working. We carry water from the pump in the yard. The iron pump is very heavy. The water supply is low. The water drips slowly into the bucket as I lift the pump with all my strength, lowering it with a groan.

"Let me help you." I hear a warm voice as two powerful arms lift the pump with ease. I turn and face my rescuer. Big, brown eyes smile at me.

"I am Moishe Senderowicz. They call me Moniek. I am from Wyszogrod."

"I am Riva Minska, from Lodz." I feel myself blush.

"Where do you stay?" His voice is strong yet gentle.

"I am staying with friends on the second floor of the building behind us."

"We are all friends here." His eyes are on my face. I lower my gaze. He picks up the bucket of water and carries it up to my apartment. "I will see you later."

We shake hands.

He returns later, bringing canned meat

and bread—a real feast that we share with all present.

"Did you go back to Wyszogrod?" I ask softly as we sit alone in the corner of the crowded room.

His eyes have a faraway look now. "I went back to Wyszogrod," he says. "I hoped to find them there, my parents, my brothers Shmuel and Berl, my aunts, uncles, cousins. But there was no one. No one left." He sighs painfully. "Only three Jews from all the Jews in Wyszogrod had returned: a girl, another boy, and I. Only three Jews. The house we owned lay in ruins. I searched in the rubble but found no trace. Not a trace of my family. They all vanished. Not a trace." He stops, takes a deep breath. "I could not remain there. I didn't even say good-bye to the others. I walked off to the train station. I did not care where the train took me as long as it took me away . . . far away. . . ."

"I, too, went back to what was once my home." My voice is just above a whisper. "I, too, left. . . . This land is soaked with our blood. We are not wanted here, even now." We sit silently, each absorbed in tormented thoughts.

"If at least one member of my family could be found, at least one . . ." His voice trails off. "When the Nazis closed us up in the ghetto of Wyszogrod in 1940, they ordered one male from each family to report for work outside the ghetto. I was seventeen, strong, so I went. After a few months of hard labor they took us back to the ghetto to exchange us for other males in our families. They wanted to take my father. I knew he could not survive that hard labor. I volunteered to go again in his place." His eyes have a faraway look again. "I never saw my family again. I was sent from the labor camp to Auschwitz. I do not even know what happened to them. . . ."

I stare at the number tattooed in blue ink on his left arm, 75087. "How long were you in Auschwitz?"

"Five years. Five years."

I gasp. "Five years! How did you survive?"

He seems to be searching for an answer. "I do not know how. I survived."

There is anger in his voice. He turns his head toward the wall, stares at the blank wall for a moment, then turns toward me again. There is a silent apology in his eyes. "I survived many work details, selections to the gas chambers. I faced castration. I faced death. I survived five years." He takes a deep breath. "Then they shipped us to a labor camp in Glajwitz. I decided then that if they put us on another train I must try to jump off while the train was in motion. It was my only chance. They might shoot me, but I had to try. The Germans were losing the war. Our end, too, was near. They kept reminding us, 'Before we go kaput, you all will be kaput.' Each day large transports from the camp were sent to unknown destinations." He swallows hard. "After liberation I heard what happened to the transports: They were sent to death.

"I spoke to another man about my plan. He wanted to come with me. We managed to steal overalls from the supply house and some sugar. We waited for our only chance to escape, the train. The orders came. We were put on an open coal train. At night, with the train in full speed, we jumped into the snow. The guards kept on shooting at us as the train sped on. We were not hit, only bruised. We hit all night, afraid that they might return to search for us."

He closes his eyes. His face reflects the terror of that night.

"We changed into the coveralls and made our way to the nearest town, Sosnowiec. At the outskirts of the town we entered a farmhouse. I told the woman we found there that we are Poles, escapees from a German labor camp. 'Our lives are in your hands,' I said.

"She gave us food. 'My husband, too, is in a German labor camp,' she told us. She cried. Believing that we were Poles, she hid us for six weeks, until the Russian army liberated the town. She would not have hidden us had she known that we were Jews. She told us often how happy she was that 'the Germans are taking care of the Jews.'"

"You were lucky that you look like a Pole. It saved your life."

He takes my hand in his. It is warm and strong. "I may look like a Pole, but I suffered as a Jew. I will always be a Jew."

nine

JULY 7, 1945. Moniek and I are married. The young man with the warm, brown eyes, with the blue number on his arm, with the pain and anger in his heart, is now my husband. It has been only five weeks since we met at the old water pump, in a German backyard. We have no time for a long courtship. We need no long courtship. We need each other. An urgent, burning need to rise from the ashes, to build again, fills our hearts and minds. We are all alone. No family to share our joy, to tell us mazel tov, congratulations. A few friends help us celebrate this special day. Joy is mixed with sadness.

Karola, Oscar, Moniek, and I move into another building abandoned by Germans when the Russians came. We enter the four-room apartment we will share and move about cautiously. I feel like an intruder about to be caught in someone else's home. The apartment is pretty and comfortable. I wonder who lived here. What did they do? Were they concentration camp guards? Did they give orders to kill, or did they follow the orders? Did they close their eyes, their ears, their minds, their hearts? Chills run down my spine.

In the kitchen Karola opens a cabinet door. She gasps. The cabinet is filled with silver goblets and silver candlesticks. She takes a goblet in her hand. "It has Hebrew writing!" she cries out. "This comes from a Jewish home!" I take another goblet from the cabinet. This, too, has a Hebrew inscription. We look around. The apartment is filled with the plundered remains of Jewish homes. Our eyes well up with tears.

I hold a goblet in my shaking hands, touching it gently. This beautiful silver goblet was used to celebrate holidays, to welcome the Sabbath. It speaks of joyous occasions. Of families. Where are they, those people who held this goblet raised in a blessing? Did they survive? Did they die in gas chambers? Did they starve to death? Did they die from German bullets? Did someone in this house contribute to their death?

I touch the remnants of destroyed lives. My hands quiver. This home is filled with the shadows of victims, with their silent cries for justice. Can I move in this place without screaming, without shouting why?

"Riva, we have no other place." Moniek reads my thoughts. "We are in the lion's den. No matter where we go, the past will follow." He takes my hand in his. "We survived. We are free. Our murderers live in fear now."

"There is no place for us," I whisper through my tears.

"We must wait here. Maybe one of the transports from Russia will bring your sisters and brother back to you." He wipes the tears from my face.

Oscar has just told me wonderful news. He has found his sister Pepa. She survived the Nazi hell and is coming to live with us.

Pepa is alive. Maybe we'll find others, too. We must hope.

The few Germans who still live in the city live in fear of Russian vengeance. The streets are full of Russian soldiers. Two German women living in our building beg to be our servants.

"The Russians leave the survivors alone. We can hide here. They may rape us. They may kill us." They plead, they cry.

I cannot look at them. Maybe they are murderers.

"We will be safer in a home of survivors. Please, we want to work for you. Please."

We feel pity. They are in danger. We must help them.

The city is in chaos. There are no jobs. We live by trading one item for another.

Moniek and I are married five months. We do not speak of it, but we all live with the hidden fear of not being able to bring forth a new generation. The survivors who were part of inhuman experiments, who were castrated, sterilized, know the horrible truth. They will forever remain childless. The others wonder. What else did the Nazis do to assure a world free of Jews?

I think back to the years in the concentration camps. Very seldom did any of the girls there menstruate. Was it malnutrition, or were there other reasons? The fear grows stronger with each month. We want a family. A new link to the future, a continuation.

"You are pregnant," the doctor I see says happily.

Moniek and I are overjoyed. A child. Our child. A new life is growing within me. But the wonderful news is marred by a notice from the Polish military. Moniek is being drafted into the army.

"I will never serve in the Polish army, Riva." Pale, shaken by the notice, Moniek marches around the room like a caged animal. "I will not leave you alone to become a soldier in a land that shows only indifference and hatred to some of its citizens, the Jews." His voice is firm, determined. "There is no place for us here. We will leave tonight."

We pack quickly.

"Where will you go?" Oscar asks, trying to sound composed.

"We will make our way back to Lodz, and from there, out of Poland," Moniek replies.

"I will keep on checking the transports. I promise." Karola hugs me tight.

"I will let the Jewish Committee in Lodz know where we are planning to go." I swallow the lump choking my throat. "We must not lose one another."

We say tearful good-byes to our friends.

Moniek takes my face in his hands. "Look at us, Riva. We came to Wroclaw as two strangers. Two lonely people. Lost souls, searching for family." His eyes glow. "We found each other. We started a new life, a family, a new generation." A loving smile plays on his lips.

I cuddle close to him.

ten

OUR FIRST STOP in Lodz is the Jewish Committee. The walls are covered with lists of names. Names of survivors. Names of people inquired about. My heart pounds violently. Quickly I search the lists. Names. Names. Names. Not one familiar name. Not one message. I stare at the faces of strangers. They stare back with eyes void of hope. I read my own painful thoughts in their dejected gazes: No one is searching for me. There is no one left to be found. I drag my feet, lumps of clay, from the office.

I wander the streets of Lodz, eyes blurred with tears. People are rushing by, searching faces as they pass, moving as if chased by an invisible force. I, too, begin to move faster. I hold Moniek's arm tight. "It feels so strange to be back again."

My husband pulls me closer to him.

"I grew up here, Moniek. I lived here with a loving family, attended school, belonged to clubs. It all seems so long ago." My eyes do not stop searching. "I am looking for traces of the childhood I left behind.

I am looking for traces of my family, of my friends." My voice rises and falls. "There are no traces to be found. But it seems only yesterday, or maybe it was another lifetime, that I walked with my friends on these sidewalks, books under our arms, a song on our lips. I still hear them singing, Moniek. I still hear their voices."

"I, too, hear voices from the past, Riva." He lowers his head. We walk silently.

Suddenly I stop, frozen to the spot. "Moniek, this is the same sidewalk I was kicked from by a German soldier shouting, 'Jew, off the sidewalk! Jews walk in the gutter!' It was right here. Right on this street."

Suddenly it is 1940 again. I hear the Germans shout. I feel the kick of a German's boot against my body. I hear my cousin Sabcia scream. I see her perplexed, angry eyes as I fall into the gutter. I see men, women, and children with yellow stars on their clothing herded into the gutter. I hear shots. I hear cries of horror.

"Riva! Are you all right?" Moniek's voice, his arm around me, brings me back to reality. It is 1945. I am free. There are no more Germans here. Jews walk freely on the sidewalks of Lodz. I hear the sound of Yiddish. It is music to my ears: It feels good to be alive. It feels good to be free.

Cultural and political groups form

again. Members of the Jewish socialist labor movement, the Bund, argue again with the members of the Zionist movement. Each group hotly, fervently defends its views.

The Bundists argue: "Jews lived in Poland for a thousand years and created a rich Jewish culture. It is all destroyed. We must remain here, rebuild from the ashes. We must bring Jewish life, Jewish culture back to Poland. We who survived have a duty to those who perished to rebuild here."

"The only home for Jews is Eretz Israel, the land of Israel," stress the Zionists. "Only Israel has a place for Jews."

Anti-Semitism, too, is alive again. The old slogans reappear.

"Do not buy from the Jew."

"Jews to Palestine."

"Kill the Jew."

Jews, survivors of Nazi death camps, are attacked in the streets, in their homes. Again Jewish blood is being spilled in Poland.

I feel fear again. I feel anger again. I feel bitterness. Again I share my anger in my poems.

World, do not cry for our dead;
we do not need your tears.
We need a place to live free.
We need a place to feel safe.
We need a home.
I stare at the words I have put on paper.

They shout at me, *You are not free. You are still in a cage.* The flames of the crematorium did not consume us. Poland is free. Yet again we are murdered, not by Nazis but by free Poles, only because we are Jews. And the world—the world only sheds tears.

We must leave Poland. We must cross borders illegally. Where do we go?

"I hear that the Americans and the British have formed camps for displaced people," a friend announces as he enters the apartment we are staying in until we can move on.

My heart beats fast. "Where?"

He does not answer.

"Where?" I ask again, impatient.

"In Germany," comes his choked reply.

"Germany? How can we go back to Germany?" My voice sounds hollow, strange. It is not my voice. It is the collective voice of all those whose blood, whose ashes fill the German soil.

A young woman screams, "Not Germany! Not Germany!"

Another woman puts her arm around her. "Calm down, dear. We must think clearly. It is life or death again."

"But Germany? That cursed land?" she shouts.

"We have no choice," someone says painfully. "We must leave Poland. We are facing death again."

Shivers run down my spine. Moniek is in danger of being caught and put into prison for evading the Polish army. We all are in danger from anti-Semitic attacks. We must leave as soon as possible—but Germany?

We leave notice at the Jewish Committee for anyone who may search for us. My hands shake as I write: "Riva Minska Senderowicz and Moniek Senderowicz are trying to make their way to the displaced persons camp in Berlin."

I stand in line at the information desk to leave my note and ask one last time if anyone is searching for me.

It is my turn. "Riva Minska, from Lodz." I tremble as I watch the young woman search her files carefully.

Then, with a cry of triumph, she pulls a postcard from her files. "For the Minski family. From Russia. It arrived only a few days ago."

My knees buckle as I take the postcard from her hand. It was mailed three months ago. I sit down to keep from falling and read: "We, Mala, Chana, and Yankl Minski are searching for members of the Minski family of Lodz." The address is of a place deep, deep in Russia. I press the card close to my lips.

I have a message. A card written by someone in my family. "Moniek, I have family. We have family," I whisper through tears of joy.

"They may be on their way back to Lodz. We are leaving. How will we ever find one another?" I search his face for an answer. He takes the card in his hands.

"Riva, there is an address here. Let's send a telegram. Let's let them know you are alive."

"But this card was mailed three months ago," I stammer. "They may not be there any longer."

"Let's send it, anyway."

We rush to the post office. I copy the strange address carefully. "I am alive. Your sister, Riva Minska," I write.

I speak to people who return from Russia. They tell of hardships in trying to come back home. Of long, long journeys. I do not know where my sisters and brother are. Did they get into a transport for Poland? Even if they did, it will take months for them to get here. If we should wait for them in Poland, Moniek might get caught. He would be put into military prison for many years. But if I leave, I might never see my family again.

I must make a choice. I look at my husband and see the agony in his eyes. I am all he has. We are beginning a new life together. He is going to be a father. How can I take a chance with his life? How can I take a chance with our lives? With the life of our unborn child?

"We must leave, darling." My voice breaks. "I must hope that somehow we will find my sisters and brother. They are alive." I hold him close.

eleven

WHEN WE CAME back from the camps, the Polish borders were open to returnees: Now the borders are closed, especially to those who wish to leave. We will have to escape.

We are told that in the border town of Szczecin we may find smugglers to bring us across the Polish-German border, which on the German side is of course under Russian rule. We board a crowded train to Szczecin. The only two empty seats are opposite a Polish officer. My heart pounds. The military uniform fills me with panic. The officer smiles politely. We sit down. His eyes wander sharply from Moniek to me. Fears grips me.

"Where are you folks going?" His voice is tense.

"We are going to visit family in Szczecin." Moniek's voice is calm.

The officer keeps watching me intensely. Slowly he turns his eyes to the window. "It is good to visit family." His eyes are on me again. "Poland is a fine country. Too bad it is still unsafe for Jews to travel." His eyes jump from me to Moniek. He lowers his voice to a whisper. "The A.K., the Polish partisan group that fought against the Germans, is unhappy to see that some Jews survived. They search trains for Jews, pull them off, and kill them." There is pity in his eyes as he looks at me. "I am a Polish officer and even I am helpless." He turns back to Moniek. "If the A.K. should stop this train, your Jewish wife will be taken off. You will never see her alive again."

"Would you let them kill her? You, an officer in the Polish army." Moniek's eyes flash with anger.

"Lower your voice," whispers the officer. He bends closer to us. "We Poles should be angry. But they'll kill us both if we interfere." He speaks to Moniek but keeps his eyes on my face. "The safest thing for Jews to do is stay off trains."

I want to scream, *Jews are not safe anywhere!* But I remain silent. I move closer to Moniek. The officer thinks Moniek is a Pole.

We arrive safely in Szczecin. Outside the train the A.K. is waiting. They scrutinize everyone. Moniek puts his arm around me.

"Is this your wife?" one of them asks.

"This is my woman." Moniek smiles broadly.

The man smiles back at Moniek and waves us on.

I read in Moniek's eyes the same

thought that runs through my mind. We have just faced death again. We were saved only by Moniek's Polish looks.

We meet others who are trying to cross the border. Moniek finds a smuggler. He agrees to take six people, hide them among the furniture on his truck. He moves the furniture only to the Russian zone of Berlin. From there we have to make our way to the American zone. He asks to be paid in advance. Moniek refuses to pay before we are in the truck. The Russian hesitates but finally agrees to wait until we are all hidden in the truck.

"I would not trust him with an advance," Moniek says as we hurry to join the others. "I heard that some of the smugglers take the money and leave you stranded. Someone always takes advantage of another's misfortune. We have to give him all the money we got from selling the things we found in the deserted German homes. I do not trust him, but we have no choice."

"We have to trust someone, sometime, Moniek."

He gives me a strange look. "You are so naive, Riva."

"Maybe I am." I feel defensive. "Maybe I am, but there has to be some compassion in people. There has to be some good in them."

We are three young couples. We squeeze in between the huge pieces of furniture. "It is only for a few hours, friends," one of our fellow travelers proclaims. "We will make it." His voice betrays his hidden fear.

"What are we going to do without money? We gave the Russian all we had," one woman asks nervously.

"When we get there alive and well, we'll worry about money." Her husband has his arm around her. "It is not the first time we are left with nothing." She sighs and nods in agreement.

The driver locks the doors of the truck. I feel panic. My heart pounds violently. I can hardly catch my breath. I cling to Moniek. I must not panic. I must calm down. I must keep in mind that it was a Russian truck driver who locked the doors, not a Nazi guard. I must remember that he is taking us away from here, to safety. It is not a concentration camp that is waiting for us on the other side. It is freedom. I must calm down.

I look at Moniek. His face is drawn and tense. I look at the others. Their faces, too, reflect their inner fears. They, too, must be remembering journeys in locked trucks, in locked cattle cars. Journeys that ended in death, left few survivors.

"We have endured worse," someone says as if answering an unspoken question.

"How will we get from Germany's Russian zone to its American zone?"

"What will happen to us if we get caught by the Poles or the Russians?"

"Do not despair, friends."

"We must hope for the best."

"I wonder what the displaced persons camp is like?"

We speak in whispers, asking questions none of us can answer. The wheels of the truck pound hard on the rough roads as they carry us forward in our desperate search for safety. The hours pass slowly. Has it been hours or years? I wonder.

"We should have been over the border by now." Someone voices his concern.

"It is taking much longer than it should." Someone else agrees.

Unspoken fear fills the stuffy air. What is wrong?

Suddenly the truck stops. The door opens. The light stings my eyes. The driver stands at the door of the truck. He looks like an animal about to devour his prey.

"Are we in Berlin?"

"Why did we stop?"

"What is wrong?"

An uncanny smile plays menacingly on the driver's lips as he studies our anxious faces. "No, we are not in Berlin. We are still in Poland, still far from the border." He stops, looks quietly at us, enjoying his power over us. "Jews, I want more money. I am taking a chance, risking prison. I want more money." He weighs the effect of his little speech. "So you give me more money now, or you can remain here, in this field."

We stare at him in horror. "We have no more money," Moniek shouts. "We gave you all the money we had. We have no more."

The driver turns toward him slowly. "Well, then, stay here. Find the border on your own."

"But how will we pass the border without being caught? Have a heart."

He shrugs his shoulders. "Give me more money or walk back."

"You cannot leave us here!" I cry.

"My wife is with child! She cannot walk back!" Moniek screams. "We gave you all the money we had." They look at each other with blazing eyes. I am afraid they will get into a fight.

"We are at his mercy, darling. Control yourself," I whisper in Yiddish. The driver stares at us angrily. "You Jews are a lot of trouble, but I feel sorry for that woman." He points at me. "Well, give me your watches, then."

We hand him the watches that we obtained in Wroclaw. He is pleased with his loot. "We are leaving for Berlin."

I hear the truck being locked again, the engine starting again. Moniek curses under his breath as we settle back among the furniture. "We will live without our watches. As long as he gets us safely over the border."

Hours later the truck stops again. Someone speaks Russian to the driver. "I have to inspect your cargo."

"Sure," the driver replies cheerfully. "It has been a long trip, comrade. Let's have a drink first. The inspection can wait."

They walk off together. We wait in painful silence. Through cracks in the truck's walls, we see that there are many trucks parked around us. From nearby, we hear the sound of drunken voices and laughter. I ache from the long, hard journey. I feel tightness in my chest. "Are we trapped? What will they do to us? Will they put us in prison?"

"Close your eyes, darling." Moniek pulls me closer. "We may stay here all ngiht. He may have gotten drunk."

"Our lives are in his hands and he gets drunk! I am too scared to sleep." I put my head in Moniek's lap. My eyelids feel so heavy. I close my eyes. The motion of the moving truck startles me. I open my eyes, look around, bewildered.

"Easy, darling, easy." Moniek holds me tight. "We are moving again. You slept all night. You must have been real worn out." Softly he caresses my face. "The driver stayed all night to drink with the others. He came back only a little while ago. He said he bribed the inspector with my watch so he would not check his cargo." He grins. "Lucky for us he had such a nice watch."

"We are near the border," someone whispers. The truck stops at the checkpoint. The driver shows his papers to the guard. It seems an eternity, but finally we cross the border.

"We are back in Germany." I hear a painful sigh.

The driver drops us off near a train station. To our surprise, he hands us some German money.

"This train will bring you to Schlachtenzay. The American zone. The displaced persons camps is located there." He disappears.

It is April 1946. Less than a year ago I left Germany. Now I am back. The train is clean and comfortable. I sit and nervously study the people around me. They all seem to be absorbed in deep thought. They ignore us. Across from me a finely dressed woman stares at me and turns her head quickly as our eyes meet. There is resentment and fear written on her face.

We reach the station. I sense relief from the other passengers as we leave the train. We wander around the station. Where do we go from here? A man is watching us from a distance. Nervously I hold on to Moniek. The stranger comes toward us. My heart beats faster.

"I will take you to the displaced persons camp," he say softly in Yiddish. "You are safe now."

"Were you waiting for us?" we ask him in disbelief.

He smiles. "For you and all the others who make it safely to this point."

twelve

THE DISPLACED PERSONS camp in Berlin has many large buildings. The camp is crowded with refugees. There are long lines for information. Long lines for registration.

We take our place in line for registration. I study the faces of those around me. The pain and horror of the past, the bewilderment of the present are written in their forever-searching eyes. Will the pain ever subside? Will we ever lead normal lives?

Lines of a poem I heard long ago suddenly run through my mind. "Everything in life slowly passes. Pain, sorrow, joy. But memories remain forever." How can we live with our horrible memories forever and not go mad? Will we have the strength, the courage to pass those memories on to the world, to future generations? I know we must pass them on.

Moniek and I are assigned a room to be shared with another couple and their child. My heart sings with joy and eager anticipation. The last time I saw a Jewish child was when they were ordered to go to the left in

Auschwitz. Those children all perished in the Nazi gas chambers. Still, there is a Jewish child in this camp. A Jewish child who survived. I feel like shouting, *A Jewish child! A Jewish child!*

We walk up a flight of stairs, through a long corridor, and stop before the door of the assigned room. A crazy thought runs through my mind: I will knock at the door and Mama will open it and enfold me in her arms again. Tears well up in my eyes.

I knock at the door gently. I swallow the lump in my throat. The door slowly opens. A dark-haired woman, about thirty, stands in the doorway. We gaze at each other silently. She smiles warmly as she extends her hand in greeting. "My name is Mania. I am from Warsaw." Her voice is soft. "You must be the couple that is to share this room with us. Welcome. Welcome."

I press her outstretched hand. "I am Riva, from Lodz. This is my husband, Moniek, from Wyszogrod."

"Oh, yes, a big city, Lodz. It had a large Jewish community." She sighs painfully. "And Wyszogrod is near Warsaw." She stops, suddenly remembering something. "Oh, yes, Wyszogrod has a magnificent synagogue." She looks at Moniek, an unspoken question in her eyes.

"It is no more. It was destroyed by the Germans." His voice is filled with pain.

"Everything destroyed," Mania murmurs.

My eyes wander around the small room, its three cots, table, and chairs. Some boxes stand in the corner.

Mania looks at my rounded belly. "They told me that you are expecting a baby. I am so happy for you." She stares at the cot. "It is not very comfortable for two . . . almost three. But it could be worse. We have a roof over our heads. There is a big dining room that we all share. You will meet people there." She sighs. "So many homeless people. They come from many places, mostly from Poland and Hungary. Some pass through. Some stay. I have been here for several months with my husband and little girl." There is a sudden painful note in her voice. "Her name is Marylka."

I sit down on the cot, my eyes on Mania. She sits in one chair, Moniek in the other. We look at one another silently.

"I know." Mania breaks the silence. "There are very few families with children. How did we survive as a family? How did we save our child?" She takes a deep breath. "We were in the ghetto of Warsaw, struggling to survive. Children were the first victims of hunger, sickness, deportation. We knew Marylka was doomed in the ghetto. We were lucky to have Christian friends outside the ghetto walls. They were willing to risk their lives to save our child. They managed to send a message into the ghetto through a mutual friend who was taken in and out of the ghetto as part of a work detail. The message was: We have found a place for the child in a convent outside Warsaw. Must act fast."

Mania's eyes fill with tears as she speaks. "A three-year-old baby. A Jewish child in a convent. I could not think of parting with my baby. But my beautiful little girl . . . her life was in our hands. How many parents in the ghetto had a chance to save their child? We had to let her go. If we should perish, our child would survive." She stops for a moment. "We parted. Our friend made a solemn promise that the convent would return Marylka to us if we lived, or to any surviving member of our families." She wipes the tears from her eyes. "Several months later we were all deported to concentration camps. I was separated from my husband. I held on to life because I knew my child was safe. I endured the horrors, the beatings. My child was waiting for me, she needed me. I had to survive. I had to find my child."

Mania is sobbing now. Moniek and I wait silently for her to calm down.

"When we were finally liberated, my first stop was the convent." Her voice is shaky. "My child was not there. I became hysterical. I wanted to die. I had nothing left to live for. A nun at the convent felt pity for me. 'I will help you search for your child, you poor soul,' she said. The dear, sweet woman. She told me that the children they had hidden in the convent had been in danger when someone reported to the Nazis that they sheltered Jewish children. They had had to send them away quickly. But she promised to help me find my child. She did."

Mania wipes her eyes again. "A peasant family had taken Marylka in. They had been told that she was a Polish orphan. I was all alone. I did not know if my husband was alive or dead. I went to claim my child from a family who had given her a home more than a year before. A family who never knew it was a Jewish child they had taken in. The kind nun came with me. When we entered the home where my child lived, my heart was about to jump out of my chest. The peasant woman became hysterical when told why we were there. 'This is not true!' she shouted. 'She is not Jewish! She is a Christian child! She is my child! Get out of here, you dirty Jew!' I felt so sorry for that woman. I still feel sorry for her. . . ."

Tears fall from Mania's eyes, glide over her cheeks and neck. Her voice is choked. "Marylka heard the shouting and came running. My child. My baby. We both froze. She stared at me for a moment, then slowly moved toward me. Her eyes, wide with horror, stared at my short crop of hair. 'Mommy, what happened to your long, pretty hair?' She fell into my arms. It had been two years. In her mind she had held on to the picture of her mommy with long, pretty hair. We held each other tight, crying. The nun cried. The peasant woman cried, too."

Mania wipes the tears from her face. "I found my husband several months later. He was very sick but alive. He said when we found each other, 'I held on to life with the last bit of strength. I knew our child was waiting. We are the lucky ones. Our child is alive and well.'"

The door opens. A man in his thirties, of medium build, with brown hair woven with gray enters. He smiles. He holds the hand of a beautiful little girl with dark, curly hair. She moves close to the man's side. She seems frightened.

Mania introduces us. "This is Leon, my husband, and this is Marylka. Leon, Marylka, this is Riva and Moniek. These people will share this room with us."

The child stares at us, uneasy. "Why do we have to share our room with strangers?"

Mania looks embarrassed. "Marylka, please, remember your manners. There are many homeless people here. We must share the room." She puts her arms around the child, hugs her. The child stiffens but does not move away from her mother's embrace.

I see a shadow crossing Leon's face as he watches the two of them. He turns quickly toward us, extending his hand in greeting. "Where are you from?"

Marylka remains at her mother's side, glancing at us with apprehension, curiosity. My heart aches for her. I have an overwhelming urge to take her in my arms. I smile at her. She moves closer to her mother. Her eyes are like the eyes of a hunted animal.

"Riva, I must show you where the bathrooms are." Mania reaches toward me, taking me by the hand. She leads me into the hall. I feel the tension in her fingers.

Shaking, she takes both my hands in hers. "I had to get you out of the room. I want to explain my child's behavior. She is very, very confused. She was so little, only three years old, when we sent her away. She lived in a different world. She was taught Catholic prayers, to cross herself, to hate Jews. She screamed, she cried as I told her that we, her mother and father, are Jews, that she is a Jewish child. She is very cold toward us. It breaks our hearts." Mania's face is a mask of agony. "But it was a terrible shock, losing her parents and then finding them again, learning she is a child of the people she was taught to hate. It will take time for her to trust us, to love us again. Do not judge my child. Be gentle. Be kind. Be patient."

I put my arms around her without a word. I feel her wet face against mine.

Marylka slowly warms toward me. I play games with her. She listens wide-eyed as I tell her children's fairy tales. She smiles as I teach her children's rhymes. I watch her as she kneels at her cot, whispers Catholic prayers, looks around her cautiously, hides her head in her hands, and cries. I cry inside as I see her confusion, her pain. I want to put my arms around her, comfort her.

"We have to let her be. Be patient," Mania says. "It will take time."

I watch her play. She seems to be in a different world. She plays with crayon and paper, drawing silently. Suddenly she stops, the crayon in midair. "Some Jews are good." She speaks to invisible people. Her voice is agitated. "My mommy and daddy are not evil. They are good." She stands up, turns toward me. "You are a Jew. You are not evil."

I reach out to her. She does not move away. She takes my hand in hers. "Are all Christians good?" Her eyes search my face, demanding an answer.

I touch her hair softly. "There are Christians who are good, and there are Christians who are bad. There are Jews who are good, and there are Jews who are bad."

There is a strange warm glow in Marylka's eyes. "I am a Jew. I am a good person."

"You are a good person, darling. You are a good person." She huddles close to me. I hold her tight. I see Mania's face wet with tears. Her eyes glide lovingly over Marylka.

thirteen

THE CAMP DINING room is the central meeting place for all who pass through here. People come to exchange the latest information on immigration rules and regulations. People come to search for family, to talk to other refugees. Heated discussions. Emotion-filled voices echo all around me.

"You must have a sponsor."

"What is a sponsor?"

"Someone to guarantee that you will not become a burden to your new country."

"How do we get sponsors?"

"Search for relatives in other countries."

"Hope for help from HIAS, the Hebrew Immigration Aid Society."

"But there are still quotas."

"Each country has its own rules, its own quotas."

"The quotas are small, the waiting lists long."

"Some countries do not want Jews."

"Who wants us?"

"The Jews in Palestine want us."

"They need us to help rebuild the barren land."

"We may perish fighting for a Jewish homeland."

"How can we get to Palestine? The British, too, set quotas."

"Illegal, secret ships travel to Palestine."

"Some of the ships never make it. They sink at sea."

"Some refugees are caught by the British and put into barbed-wire camps again."

"Again camps . . ."

"I cannot risk my life and that of my wife. We have suffered enough."

"Palestine is the only land that wants us."

"We must resist the British and Arabs and reclaim our homeland."

"But I am not a Zionist."

"But you are a Jew."

Excited voices. Angry voices. They pound in my head. I am a Jew, but do I have the courage to undertake that long, dangerous journey on overcrowded, old vessels, moving secretly, slowly, toward Palestine? Would I have the strength to face another barbed-wire cage if captured?

Moniek, too, is absorbed in painful thoughts. The agony is written all over his face. He puts his arm around me. "Were I alone I would gladly risk my life for a homeland. For a place where no one could shout, *Jew, get out.* But I must think of you, of our unborn child. You are all I have. I cannot risk losing you."

"A place where no one calls, *Jew, get out,*" I repeat slowly. "I know what you mean. Poland never had a place for us. I wish my parents had left Poland when my father's brother and sisters left for Argentina. That was before I was born. Many times Mama told me how they pleaded with my parents to leave Poland. My father wanted to go, but Mama would not part with her family. My family would have been alive today." I fight back my tears.

"All our lives would have been different had we known. But even if we had known, would we have believed?" Moniek sighs.

"I have family in Argentina, Moniek." I raise my voice and lower it again. "The first time I felt the Nazi boots on my body, I was on my way to the post office to mail a letter to our family in Argentina. The Nazis rounded up the Jews in the street. They chased us, a caravan of horror, through the streets all day. I never mailed the letter. They locked us up in the ghetto. I must remember my family's address. I must think of the address."

I close my eyes, trying hard to recall an address I had read as a child. "Emma Strauss. Emma Strauss." My lips move slowly. "Tucuman 236. Santiago del Estero. Republica Argentina. That is the address. I remember the address!" I shout. "I remember the address! I can write to them now."

I write in Yiddish. I write to my family. The family I know only from letters, pictures, gifts. My hands shake.

Dear Aunt Emma,

My name is Riva Minska. I am the daughter of your brother Avrom. With pain in my heart I write these words. Your dear sister-in-law Nacha perished in the Nazi gas chambers. My brother Laibele died in the ghetto. His grave is in the cemetery in Lodz, where my father is buried. The last time I saw my brothers Motele and Moishele was at the gates of the death camp Auschwitz. I do not know what happened to them. I survived the concentration camps, returned home to Lodz. But there was no one there. My sisters, Mala and Chana, and my brother Yankl had escaped to Russia. I found a postcard from them before my husband and I escaped Poland and came to the displaced persons camp in Germany. I hope that what is left of our family will be reunited someday.

I stop, read the words I have just put on the paper before me. I stare at the words, *Your dear sister-in-law Nacha perished in the Nazi gas chambers.* Is this real or a nightmare? This is my mother I am talking about. I bury my face in my hands.

Moniek strokes my hair. I look at him through tear-blurred eyes. "Mama's love for her family kept her in Poland even under the Nazis. Her brother Baruch, who had escaped to Russia, sent smugglers to take us over the border. The ghetto was not locked up yet. Mama refused to leave. 'We must hold on to our home,' she argued. 'My children, my brother, my sister lost their homes. They must have a place to return to from Russia. This will soon be over. I am a widow with four young children. What would the Germans do to us? I lived under the Germans in World War I. It was hard, but they did not harm us. What could happen to us?' Moniek, I still hear her words, 'What could happen to us?'"

My husband just holds me.

I wander around the camp, looking at strangers' faces. Strangers look at my face. A woman passes by slowly, then turns, stops, and stares at me. "You are Minska," she says matter-of-factly. "You look like your sister Chana. I worked with her and your sister Mala in the same factory in Russia."

Speechless, I stare at her. My eyes well up with tears.

"Do not cry, dear. They are alive."

"I found a postcard from them before I left Poland. It was mailed months before." I can hardly speak. "How did they look when you saw them?"

"They looked like the rest of us. Hungry, worn out. But alive."

"How about my brother? Did you see my brother?"

"No. He was sent to a different workplace."

"You saw my sisters. You saw my sisters," I mumble in disbelief.

She puts her arm around me. "I am glad I can bring happy news to someone. Something pushed me to visit this camp today. I was destined to be a bearer of good news. They'll come back soon. You'll see."

New people arrive. Others leave. The arrivals are met with eager eyes, fervent questions. A spark of hope. The pain of disappointment. Some depart for other countries. They are sent off with wishes for good luck. I wonder if we will ever be so lucky. Will we find a sponsor? Will we find a place to go? We must hope.

"My mother had a sister in America," Moniek says as we stare out the window aimlessly. "Her name was Borenstein. She lived somewhere near Boston. I might have family in America. If only I could find them. How do we search for them?"

How do we search? echoes in my ears. Searching, always searching. We search for traces of family. We search for unknown relatives in faraway lands. Flickers of hope keep us going. We must build a new life.

How? Where? We cannot remain in Germany.

Inside the displaced persons camp we are in a world apart. Among the survivors we share the same agony, the same hope. But outside, outside is Germany. Each time I go outside the camp, I shudder. I stare at the Germans I pass and wonder, Is this man with the self-assured, cold face a murderer? Did he send my family to death? Was this elegant lady with the dog at her side a Nazi guard? What terrible secrets do they hide in their hearts? Do they know what happened to my family?

Moniek returns one day from meeting new arrivals. "I met someone I know from Wroclaw." His voice is choked. "He told me that after we left Wroclaw someone came to ask for me."

"Who was it?" I gasp.

"He said it was a young man named Shmuel." Tears fill his eyes. "It may have been my older brother, Shmuel. I must search for him."

"Did he leave a message?" The words rush from my mouth.

"Yes. He is making his way to München, Germany. He is trying to get to Palestine from there."

Moniek takes my hand. "We must move on. I am sorry. I know we were going to stay here and wait to hear from your sisters and brother. We left a message for them in Lodz that we are trying to get to Berlin." His face reflects the anguish inside of him. "We must ask the office of the camp here to ship us to the displaced persons camp in München as soon as possible. I must find my brother before he moves on."

I take my husband in my arms. "We will leave a message here that we are going to München, my love. We must not wait." I swallow my tears.

fourteen

WE ARE ASSIGNED a place in one of the huge barracks at the displaced persons camp in München. I gasp as we enter. Suddenly it is Auschwitz again. Long layers of bunks cover the walls. Pain-filled eyes stare at us from the wooden cubicles. I want to scream, but I cannot utter a sound. I grab Moniek's hand.

"Are you all right? Riva, this is only a transit camp. We will not be here long." His eyes wander around the crowded barrack. "This is like a concentration camp," he mumbles, tightening his fingers around my hand. He leads me to an empty bunk. "Rest for a while, Riva. I must ask if anyone has met my brother Shmuel." His voice quivers with hope.

"Check the lists again, Moniek," I urge.

"I will. I will."

I watch him walk off and vanish in the crowd. Instantly panic grips me. The faces of my brothers Motele and Moishele float before me. Tears stream down my face. They, too, swallowed by a crowd, disappeared from my side. They never came back.

"Moniek is safe," I whisper. "We are free."

Despondent, Moniek returns hours later. He sits heavily on the bunk, stares silently at the people around us. I touch his face gently.

"I was so sure I would find him here." He bows his head.

"Do not give up, Moniek. Hope of finding family alive helped us survive the Nazi hell. We must not lose hope now. 'As long as there is life, there is hope.' My mother repeated those words often. I draw strength from them."

I hold his face in my hands. He kisses my fingers.

"As long as there is life, there is hope," he repeats.

Weeks pass. Moniek spends the day searching. There is no trace of Shmuel. He was never registered in this camp. No trace of anyone we search for. It is as if they had never lived.

Newspaper people. Military people. People from different relief organizations. They move through the barracks. Their eyes reflect their horror, their pity. They ask questions gently, cautiously.

"What was it like in the camps?"

"What did the Nazis do to you?"

"How did you survive?"

"Did you find family?"

"Where are you from?"

Their cameras capture the misery, the sparks of hope. They promise to print the pictures, to tell the stories of horror. The stories of courage. The stories of hope.

"Print my name, too." A woman pleads with an American newspaperman. "I had family in America. Maybe someone will recognize my name."

They leave for home. We remain in camp. Remain to search for a place *we* can call home. We spend our days searching for familiar faces, listening for the sound of familiar voices, asking questions. No sign of anyone.

"Riva, we are being sent to another displaced persons camp, in Pocking, Germany. I was told it is not as crowded as this camp." Moniek sits at the edge of the bunk. "I did not find my brother here. I was so full of hope when we came." He stares at his clenched hands. "So full of hope. Maybe in another place. . . ."

fifteen

THE DISPLACED PERSONS camp in Pocking looks much like the one in München—like the concentration camps I was caged in. I swallow the lump that forms in my throat. One thought keeps pounding in my head: *Remember, you are free.*

A young woman lets us into the room we are assigned to share. She, too, is expecting a baby. I extend my hand in greeting. "We are Riva and Moniek Senderowicz. I am from Lodz. Moniek is from Wyszogrod."

"You are from Poland." She takes my hand. "We are from Budapest, Hungary. I am Magda Unger, and this is my husband, David." Her eyes rest on my belly. "We are bringing a new generation into this world. They will have no grandparents to cradle them, but they will help us rebuild our lives." Her voice is warm and confident.

Her husband looks at her with pride. "My Magda is just wonderful. Full of hope for the future, even in this place."

Again I note meager surroundings: two cots, a table, a few chairs, a small stove.

"David!" Magda scolds him softly. "Do not sin. Do not complain. We are alive. God is with us."

David lowers his head like a scolded child. "I will not sin by complaining. God sent me you. He *must* be with us."

Moniek smiles, shaking hands with our new roommates. "Riva and Magda will get along fine. They are both strong on hope."

I feel drawn to these people. Their gentleness, their warmth were not destroyed by the horror, the degradation, the suffering. Their faith in God, their faith in humanity endured.

Magda and I talk constantly—about our childhood, our struggle to survive, our hope for the future.

"David and I are the only survivors in our families." She sighs. "Only two from all those relatives we had in Hungary. We found relatives in America. They were happy, very happy to hear that someone survived." Tears glisten in her eyes. "They are going to sponsor us. It takes a long time. It is very complicated, but, God willing, we will go to America. I hope it is before my baby is born." She takes a deep breath. "I hope my baby will be born in America, not here. Not in Germany."

"I know how you feel, Magda." I take her hand in mine. "I, too, want my child to be born in America, the land of freedom.

But if it should not be, I will still be filled with joy that we are here to bring a new Jewish generation into the world. Just think of it, Magda!" I press her hand. "Just think! Hitler did not succeed in his plan to annihilate our people. The Nazi death machine is destroyed, and right here, right here on Germany's blood-soaked soil, we, the survivors, give life to a new Jewish generation."

"It is a miracle, Riva. It is a miracle."

The Joint Distribution Committee and many other relief organizations send food and clothing. We are free to do our own cooking. The tea kettle steaming on the small stove makes the room feel cozy. Magda serves tea and cake. "I baked it myself," she says proudly. There is a pretty pink color in her cheeks now. She looks like a little girl having a tea party. I, too, feel like a little girl playing house.

"Would you like more cake, Riva? It feels so good to bake." She puts another slice on my plate without waiting for an answer. "We never had a chance to learn how to cook or bake, Riva."

I nod in agreement.

"First we were too young. Then there was nothing to cook. All those horrible years we dreamed of bread. . . ." She sits down next to me. "It feels good to bake now."

sixteen

ONE DAY I see a Yiddish newspaper on the table in the canteen. The bold black letters proclaim it the *Jewish Daily Forward*. I pick up the newspaper that came all the way from America. My hands shake. I stare in amazement at the Yiddish print. "A Yiddish newspaper," I whisper.

At that moment I see Mama pushing piles of Yiddish newspapers frantically into the fire of the coal oven. Her voice trembles. "Hurry, children. We must burn these newspapers before the Germans come."

My eight-year-old brother, Moishele, looks at her. "Mama, what are you doing?" he shouts. "Why are you burning Daddy's newspapers?"

Mama, her face flushed, tears streaming down her cheeks, turns toward him. Her eyes meet those of her youngest child. "My poor, poor baby. You were born a few months after your father's death. He died so suddenly, so young." She looks at the burning fire. "You know him only from pictures, from what you have heard about him, from the newspapers he wrote for." Her trembling hands keep pushing the newspapers into the flames. "Now we must burn the thoughts he left behind. We must burn the newspapers, for his words may put us in danger. He wrote political satire, spoke against the Nazis." She rips a newspaper into shreds. "Forgive me, my children. I am thinking of your safety."

I stare at the Yiddish letters in front of me as if they had returned from the flames to bring my father's legacy back to me. I turn the pages of the newspaper cautiously, afraid they might disappear into flames — like my father's words, like my loved ones.

Someone leans over my shoulder. "I see you read Yiddish. I looked at the paper before, and there are so many English words in it, one can learn English from the Yiddish newspaper."

I turn my head and come face-to-face with a middle-aged man with smiling pale blue eyes. He points at a word in the newspaper. "Well, read this," he challenges. I read the word he is pointing to, but it makes no sense.

"Well, you see what I mean." He smiles triumphantly. "Seems to me that the Jews in America speak half Yiddish, half English."

We sit down at the table before us.

"My name is Meyer. I know some English. I could teach you so you'll find it easier to read the Yiddish newspaper." There is a ring of playfulness in his voice. His tired face is covered with a warm grin.

"My name is Riva." I extend my hand in greeting. "You are funny, Mr. Meyer." I smile.

He takes my hand, gives it a friendly squeeze. "It is time we found something to smile about. And don't call me Mr. Meyer. I am not that old. Just call me Meyer."

Together we read the newspaper silently, each waiting for the other to finish the page before we turn it over.

"My dear wife used to read the newspaper with me like this. She is gone. Perished with our little son and daughter." He stops. "I am all alone now. All alone. Life goes on. . . ."

I press his hand. He holds my hand gently in his. "Life goes on. I do not know where our strength comes from." He stares at the newspaper, but his thoughts seem to be in another world.

My heart aches for him. For the ones he lost. For his empty, lonely world.

Suddenly a familiar name stares back at me from the pages of the newspaper. Froiem Zelmanowicz. I gasp. He was a prominent leader of the Jewish socialist labor movement, the Bund, in Lodz. I must write to him. He might not remember me—I was a child—but he knew my family well. Maybe he can help find Moniek's family in

America. I will write in care of the *Jewish Daily Forward*. I copy the address: 175 East Broadway. New York. U.S.A.

I rush to my room, holding tightly my newfound treasure, a name from the past. I write:

Dear Froiem Zelmanowicz,

My name is Riva Minska. I am a daughter of your friends Avrom and Nacha Minski. I saw your name in the Jewish Daily Forward, which reached us here in the displaced persons camp in Pocking, Germany. I am so happy to learn that you survived. I am the only member of my family to survive the ghetto, death camp, labor camp. My older sisters and brother escaped to Russia. I hope to find them again soon.

We, my husband and I, must turn to you for help. To be able to emigrate from here we must have a sponsor. My husband, Moniek Senderowicz, had family in Boston. Their name is Borenstein. Could you please find a way to trace his family in America. I am sorry we do not have much information to give you, only the name and the area where they lived. I am not sure if they still live there. I know that you will do all you can to help. Thank you so much.

Be well.

Riva Minska Senderowicz

My heart beats fast. Our fate is tied to this short letter. Will this letter reach Froiem

Zelmanowicz in America? Will the newspaper know where to contact him? Will he be able to find Moniek's family?

I feel drained. I rest my head on the table.

seventeen

SEVERAL MONTHS HAVE passed since I wrote to Froiem Zelmanowicz in America. Still I have not heard from him. I wonder if the letter ever reached him. I feel let down, forgotten. I see the same pain in Moniek's eyes. We had a ray of hope that slowly vanished. *Where shall I go? All the doors are closed to me.* A now-familiar song buzzes in my head. *Where shall I go?*

Magda and David will be leaving for America soon. Their baby will be born in America. I am very happy for them. But soon we, too, will part. A sharp pain cuts through me. We will be alone again.

A neighbor calls through the open door. "Riva, I just came from the camp post office. There is a package there for you. A package from America." He smiles, pleased to bring some good news.

"From America? I have no family in America." I stare at him. "Are you sure?"

"Yes, yes. From America, for you. It is from a Jewish relief organization. Go. Go," he urges. "Seems that someone knows you are here."

I rush to the post office.

"From America." The clerk smiles as he hands me a small brown box. "You are lucky."

I rush back to my room. My hands shake as I rip the box open. I look inside and gasp. The box is filled with delicacies: cocoa, tea, candies, cookies, jam. The last time I drank cocoa was in 1939 with my brothers and sisters. We were still a family. That was a lifetime ago.

Tucked neatly between the packages in the box is an envelope: To Riva Minska from Froiem Zelmanowicz.

My dear Riva,

Your letter was given to me only yesterday. It wandered from place to place. It found me here at the Jewish relief organization. I packaged this box myself for the daughter of my friends Avrom and Nacha. My heart goes out to you. I cried bitterly as I read your letter. I cry as I write this note. I shed endless tears for those who perished so tragically. I shed endless tears for our world that is no more.

I receive many requests from people who knew me in Lodz to help find families in America. I try to help. I want to assure you, dear child, that I will do all I can to locate your husband's family. I will put the information you sent me in the Jewish newspapers. They run lists of names of people searching for family, for friends. Let's hope for good results. You survived. Do not lose your courage now. Do not lose hope. You are not forgotten.

Be well.

Your friend, Froiem Zelmanowicz

There is hope again. I feel the new life stirring within me. I smile through my tears. Life is worth living.

Magda and David are leaving. We embrace in our last good-bye. Gently Magda wipes the tears from my face. With only our lips we wish each other mazel, luck. They walk out. The room suddenly becomes big and empty. Will I ever see them again?

No other people are assigned to our room because the baby is due soon. The camp has a medical barrack and a midwife to assist in the birth of a child. I am happy that I do not have to go to a German hospital. Now more than ever I wish I had family near me. I still do not know where my sisters and brother are. I informed the Jewish Committee in Lodz each time we moved from one camp to another. But there is no news.

"No news is good news." Moniek holds me close.

I know he, too, is thinking of his brothers. It has been over a year since our liberation. The only spark of hope, the news that someone had asked for him in Wroclaw, is beginning to die. This may have been a case of mistaken identity, of wrong information. It happens so often now. Still we must hope.

"No news is good news." I echo Moniek's words.

eighteen

I SIT ON a bench in front of our barrack, crocheting doilies for our table. The warm summer breeze caresses my face. I close my eyes, inhale the fresh air deeply. It is wonderful to be free. I do not take freedom for granted now that I have found it again.

A young woman sits down next to me. Her light brown hair hangs softly around her pale face. Her eyes are red from crying.

"My name is Riva. I am from Lodz." I extend my hand.

She turns sharply toward me. "My husband is from Lodz. He is going back to Poland. He was told that his brother is alive and in Lodz." The words rush from her mouth. "He is going back to Poland to bring his brother here."

Our eyes meet. I see the fear, the agony that fills them.

"We were about to leave on an illegal ship for Palestine when he got the news. He will not leave until he is reunited with his brother."

"It is a hard and dangerous journey. No

wonder you are upset." I sigh. "I did hear that someone is going back to Poland. You said your husband is from Lodz. What is his name?"

She wipes the tears from her eyes. "Avrom Goflat. His brother's name is Moniek. They lived on Brzezinska Street."

My head spins. I hold on to the bench with both hands to keep from falling. She puts her arm around me. "Are you all right? You turned so pale, as if you were about to faint."

I gasp for air. "Moniek Goflat was my friend. He died in the ghetto."

She stares at me. "Are you sure?"

"I was at his funeral."

She jumps up and begins to run, then turns toward me, pleading, "Do not go away. Please wait here. Please wait here."

She returns quickly. A handsome man in his late twenties with sandy blond hair is by her side. I have not seen him for seven years. He escaped to Russia. He looks like his brother, Moniek. He is trying to recall my name.

"I am Riva Minska. I came often to your house."

His eyes light up. He grabs my hands. "I remember you now. You went to school with my brother, Moniek. Your uncle Baruch Grundman was my teacher. I attended the same school, the Wladimir Medem Shul." He embraces me warmly. "It is so good to see a familiar face." His face is radiant. "It is good to see a friend of my brother's. He is in Lodz. I am going back there to bring him out. Together we will go to rebuild our homeland, Israel."

I feel as if two steel arms are pressing my throat, keeping me from breathing. I look at his wife. She shakes her head. No, she did not tell him.

My knees buckle under me. I sit down heavily on the bench. He sits down next to me.

"Avrom." My voice is very low. "Avrom. Your brother is—" I cannot find the words.

"What about my brother?"

"Avrom, your brother did not survive. He died in the ghetto of Lodz. He had dysentery."

His eyes fill with anger, horror. "No! No! That is not true! He is alive! He is alive! Someone saw him in Lodz. He is alive!" he shouts wildly.

I put my arms around him. "Avrom, I wish it were true." My voice breaks. "Avrom, I was at his funeral. I held your mother in my arms as I hold you now."

He buries his face in his hands, moaning, sobbing. His wife takes him and puts her arms around him, holding him close. He lifts his head again, studies my face as if waiting for me to tell him that it is all a terrible mistake. I lower my eyes.

"Tell me about my mother, Riva." There

is an urgency in his voice. "Tell me about my mother. Did you see her often? I always felt guilty that I left. But how were we to know?" His eyes remain glued to my face.

"In the beginning I saw her often. She spoke of you all the time. She was very proud of you. She held on to life, waited for the day of your return. Then it became hard to keep track of one another, with deportation, starvation, death. We lost track. . . ."

He buries his face in his hands again. Like a wounded animal he wails. "Nothing left. They all perished." He turns to his wife. He trembles. "There is no reason to go back to Poland anymore." His voice is strained. "You, my darling, were ready to remain here all alone and let me go back to Poland as long as there was hope of finding my brother." He holds on to her hand. "We have nothing to wait for now. Nothing left. Nothing is holding us back now. We must try to get to Israel. Just the two of us."

I feel the salty taste of tears in my mouth. Avrom lived with hope until I shattered it with the terrible truth. Is it better to live with false hope, as most of us do, or to know the horrible truth?

nineteen

DID MY SISTERS and brother manage to leave Russia? Did they reach Poland? It is such a long, hard journey from Leninabad, the region in Russia from which they sent the postcard. Are they safe in Poland? Will we find one another again? The waiting is so difficult. But I am lucky to have family to wait for.

I dream of the day when we will meet again. I was only thirteen when we said good-bye. I am twenty now, married and soon to be a mother. Seven years. Seven horrifying years.

I wonder what their lives have been like. Have they managed to stay together as a family? What kind of work have they had to do?

From those who returned from Russia I have heard of the hunger, hard work, loneliness they suffered. But there were no gas chambers. No death camps.

I make daily visits to the camp post office. As always, it is filled with people eagerly awaiting some good news: a letter from a relative, a sponsor to help them leave Germany.

The young woman behind the counter smiles at me. "Riva, you have mail." She hands me a thin, light blue air mail envelope. "It is from Argentina. Do you have family there?"

"My father's family is in Argentina. I wrote to an address I remembered from my childhood. I was not even sure it was the right address."

"It must have been. I am happy for you, Riva."

Carefully I open the letter. It is written in Yiddish.

My dear, dear niece Riva,

We received your letter and are overjoyed to hear from you. It is a miracle that you survived.

I read the letter again and again. Tears blur my eyes. The horrendous, staggering words stare at me from the letter, but I refuse to believe what they say. My dear sister-in-law, Nacha, the warm, loving Nacha, perished in the Nazi gas chambers. We heard rumors. We believed they were only rumors. They said the Jews in Europe were being exterminated. We refused to believe those horror stories. The Germans are such a cultured people, we insisted. Nacha is a widow with young children. What would the Germans do to her? Why would they want to harm children? The stories about atrocities against innocent people cannot be true. The world would not allow it, I kept telling myself.

We are devastated. Our pain and outrage cannot be put into words. I think of you day and night, my poor child. I think of what you must have endured and wish I could put my arms around you and ease your pain. I hope to hold you in my arms one day. We will do everything in our power to bring you out of Germany. I checked with the immigration offices. Their laws are very strict, no room for compassion. But let's not give up.

Please let me know what you need in food, clothing to make your life in the displaced persons camp easier. You have here aunts, uncles, cousins. We are all eager to help. We hope to see you soon. Give my love to your husband. I find it hard to think of you as a married woman, not a child. I am glad you are not alone. Be well. Be strong, my darling. Best wishes from everyone in the family here.

With all my love,
Your Aunt Emma

My dear Riva. What great news! I just received a letter from your brother Yankl. Your sisters and your brother are out of Russia. I am overjoyed. They have found a message from you. Love, Aunt Emma

I rush back to the barrack, the letter

clenched in my hands. Tears of joy, of relief, stream over my face.

"Moniek, they are out of Russia! They are out of Russia!" I shout. "They know that I survived." I run into his outstretched arms.

twenty

"I THINK WE should go over to the medical barrack, Moniek." I nudge my husband. "Wake up. I think it is time."

He jumps up. "Is the baby coming? Let's go. Let's go." He runs toward the door.

"I think you should put on some clothes, Moniek."

He stops, embarrassed, quickly puts on his pants and reaches for me. "I'll carry you."

"I can walk, sweetheart. I can walk." I try to hide my nervousness.

"But is it safe to walk? I'll carry you." His voice is tense.

"It is safe." I put my arm in his. "The baby does not come that fast."

"But this is your first baby. How do you know how fast it comes?"

I smile as he leads me slowly, like an invalid. "My wife is having a baby! Call the midwife!" he shouts as we enter the medical barrack.

The nurse on duty takes my hand. "Calm down, sir. She will be all right." As she leads me into a small room and helps me gently into the bed, she mumbles under her breath, "The husbands are more trouble than the expectant mothers."

Within moments another woman enters. About forty, her graying hair pulled to the back of her head, she moves quickly toward me. A soft smile plays on her lips, but her blue eyes remain serious. "My name is Cima. I am the midwife." She puts her hand on my belly. "Relax, dear, relax. It will all be over soon. Relax. I have delivered many babies before."

"I am scared, Cima."

"You will be fine, Riva. Is this your first?" She examines me. "Well, this one will still take some time. First babies are some-times lazy." She helps me up. "You may go back to your barrack, Riva. You will be more comfortable in your room."

She opens the door. Moniek is in the doorway. "You may take your wife back to your room. There is still lots of time. This barrack is very crowded. Besides, she will be more at ease in her room with you hold-ing her hand." She smiles.

"Is it safe to take her back?" Moniek's voice betrays his anxiety.

"It is safe. It is safe."

We are back in our room but too tense to go back to sleep. Moniek holds my hand. "I hope it is a boy. We'll name him Laibele, after my father." It sounds like a plea. "After my father."

It is the Jewish custom to name a child after a deceased relative, so that the name will live on and the person who passed away will be remembered. But this name should have belonged to an old man, a great-grandfather, not one's young father. Moniek's father should have been here to see his first grandchild, to cradle him in his arms. He perished in the Nazi gas chambers. Now my first child, if it is a boy, will be named after him. His grandfather will be only a name to him.

"If it is a girl, we will name her Chava, after your mother." My voice quivers.

Moniek wipes the tears from his eyes. "The second child we'll name after your father or mother."

I pull back. "One at a time. One at a time. The first one is not born yet. Let it first be born, strong and healthy."

Moniek smiles. "It will be."

It has been three days since the start of my labor pains. Moniek is very tense. He watches my every move. Each time I grimace he rushes me back to the medical barrack.

"Do something, Cima," he pleads with the midwife. "Help her."

"There is nothing to be done, Moniek. When the baby is ready, it will be born. Everything is normal. Trust me."

There is a quiet strength about her that makes me relax.

"You go home, Moniek. Your wife will be fine." She pushes him slowly out of the room. "Go. Go home."

Moniek leaves the room but remains in the hallway all night. Each time Cima opens the door, he pokes his head in. "How are you feeling, darling?"

"Don't you have a room, a bed? You stayed all night on the hard bench in the hallway! I only deliver babies. I do not treat husbands." Cima's voice is full of compassion. "Go home. Get some rest. Riva and the baby will need you later."

Moniek lingers a while longer, then slowly leaves.

The labor pains are getting stronger. Cima wipes the perspiration from my face. "It will not be much longer, dear. You can do it, Riva." Her hands feel strong and gentle. I am grateful for her presence.

Suddenly there is a soft knock at the door. Cima opens the door. Moniek, his face flushed, stands in the doorway waving an envelope.

"I asked you to go home, Moniek. What are you doing here again?" Cima reprimands in a low voice.

"I could not stay in the empty room. I went to the post office. I do not know why. Maybe because Riva always goes there. But I am glad I did."

Moniek's eyes shine with excitement. "I have a letter for Riva. It is important." He hands Cima the envelope.

"Your wife is in labor. This is no time to read a letter." She is annoyed.

"Cima, please give her the letter." His voice is strange. "Cima, it is from her sister. The first letter after all these years."

"Cima, please let me see the letter," I beg.

She takes the letter from his hand. "Your wife is doing fine. Go. Go." She closes the door softly, hands me the letter. "You have a crazy husband, Riva. Now he wants you to read a letter." She sighs. "We are all a little crazy."

I stare at the return address on the envelope: Chana Minska, Linz, Austria. My heart pounds like a drum. Is it real? She is out of Poland. I clench the letter in my hands as the labor pains take over and ease up again. I take a deep breath and read.

My dear, dear sister Riva,

Mala, Yankl, and I were overjoyed to find a message from you at the Jewish Committee in Lodz. To know that you survived, that someday we will be together again, gives us new strength. The Jewish Committee had no other names of survivors of our family. I cannot believe, I will never believe that Mama, our dear Mama, our darling brothers, Motele, Laibele, and Moishele are gone. I want to believe it is only a horrible nightmare, that I'll soon wake up and find our family alive and well.

Mala and Yankl are still in Poland. They are searching for a way to get out. You know it is complicated and dangerous, especially with a child.

I have some happy news. I got married. His name is Moishe Weintraub. He is also from Lodz. We were smuggled out of Poland in a truck that was supposed to be moving cattle. We marched on foot through swamps and forests. It was an ordeal I will never forget. But we made it to Austria. From here we will go to Germany.

I am so anxious to see you again, to hold you in my arms. I hope Mala and Yankl will come soon. I still think of you as the little girl I left behind seven years ago. Riva, we lost seven years of our lives. I cannot think of you as a married woman.

The displaced persons offices here are just as eager to reunite families as we are to be together. They will try to help us. I hope you are well and that we will see each other soon.

With all my love,
Your sister Chana

Tears pour from my eyes. Cima wipes my face. "Are you in a lot of pain?"

"Cima, I will see my sister again. I will see my sister again." I laugh and cry.

"I am very happy for you, very happy," she says.

A sudden sharp pain grasps me. I scream. The door opens quickly. Moniek is in the doorway again. "What can I do to help?" he asks anxiously.

"I cannot keep him out of here," Cima murmurs, chasing him out once more. She walks toward me, then turns back briskly to the door and opens it. Moniek is standing behind the door. "Moniek, your wife has a sudden craving for applesauce."

He just looks at her.

"You can help now. Go home and make her some fresh applesauce." There is urgency in her voice. "An expectant mother must get what she craves."

Moniek rushes off. Cima giggles. "Well, that should keep him out of my hair for a while. It takes time to peel apples, if he has some, then cook them."

She is very pleased with her ingenuity. I smile faintly. My mind is on the letter again. Why did Chana write that Mala and Yankl are in Lodz but not mention Mala's husband, Laibish Holtzman?

Mala and Laibish were married shortly before the Nazis attacked Poland. They escaped to Russia together. Why didn't Chana mention his name? In the last letter we had from them, before all the mail to the ghetto was stopped, Mala wrote that she was expecting a baby. She enclosed a picture of herself. I can still see Mama as she read the letter again and again, kissing the picture of her oldest child. I can still hear her whisper through her tears, *My poor child, having a baby in a faraway place, all alone. I should be at her side.*

Mama, she is not alone, I told her. *She is with her husband, sister, brother. Think of it, Mama, you are going to be a grandmother. I will be an aunt. They will return soon, you'll see, and bring the baby with them.*

The ghetto was shut off from the outside world. We never heard from them again. Mama perished without seeing her first grandchild.

The letter I clench in my shaking hands now mentions a child, but not Laibish. His name was not on the postcard I found at the Jewish Committee in Lodz, either. Why? I feel a tightness in my chest. I find it hard to breathe.

Cima bends over me. She takes the letter from my hand. "Riva, calm down, please. Concentrate on your baby. It will soon be here. Calm down, please."

The door opens. Moniek rushes in with a jar of applesauce in his hands. "Here. Here is the applesauce. I had some already made in the room. I did not take too long, did I?" His eyes move quickly from Cima to me. "Riva, how are you doing? Eat. Eat the applesauce you craved."

Cima grins. "I tried to get rid of you. Well, it did not work. Riva is doing fine. You wait outside. I'll call you in as soon as the baby is born." She opens the door. "Now go, and, Riva, you listen and follow my instructions. With mazel, it will be over soon."

The first cry of my baby fills the room. Moniek is at my side instantly. The baby's cry was his cue to enter.

"It is a boy." Cima beams. "A healthy-looking boy."

"We have a son, darling, a son!" Moniek shouts with joy.

Cima cleans the baby. I gaze with wonder at the miracle before me. I whisper happily, "My child. My child."

Cima wraps the baby in a blanket, puts him into my arms. He looks at me with wide-open eyes, and my heart sings within me.

"Now the paperwork." She takes a pad in her hands. "Let's see. Today is August 27, 1946. Mazel tov. A very special day." Her eyes are filled with tears. "A very special day. A new Jewish child came into this world."

"Thank you for being here for me, Cima. Thank you." My eyes remain fixed on my baby. "My little boy."

Suddenly I gasp. "Today is August 27? Moniek, Cima." I stop to catch my breath. "Is it possible? Is it August 27?"

They stare at me. "Yes, it is," they reply in one voice.

"On August 27, 1944, I arrived in the cattle cars at the gates of hell — Auschwitz. Two years ago today I was sent to die. Yet I lived and gave birth to a child. A Jewish child. August 27. It is a miracle. A miracle."

Cima wipes the tears from her eyes. "Each one of us is a miracle."

twenty-one

FROM THE MANY barracks in the camp, people I have never met come to see the new baby. They bring small gifts, love, good wishes. They lend a hand. I am grateful for their presence, for their attention. I look at their faces filled with enchantment and tenderness as they touch the baby, and marvel at those emotions that survived horror, death, degradation. I see the agony in the eyes of those who lost children in the Nazi gas chambers. I think of the pain, the emptiness they must live with, and I cry. I hope they will find the strength to build a new life.

Moniek's world revolves around his little family. He pampers me. He washes the baby's diapers and irons them so they will be soft and smooth. He sits at the side of the cot as I nurse the baby, studies in amazement the miracle of our lives, our baby. I wonder how such a tiny baby can bring so much sunshine into our pain-filled hearts. If only we had family to share our joy with. . . .

I think of the letter I wrote to my sister Chana. I told her that I am a mother. That her first letter arrived as I was in labor, as a new life was beginning. I told her how eagerly I am awaiting the day that will reunite us again, the day she will hold my baby in her arms. I have so much I want to say, but I cannot put it into words. Will I ever be capable of talking about these years? The survivors of the concentration camps seldom speak about their experiences. It is easier to keep silent.

Then Chana and Moishe receive permission to transfer to Pocking, and before I know it Chana and I are locked in an embrace. We whisper each other's name, hold on tight, afraid to let go. Am I dreaming? Is she really here? Will she be gone again if I let her out of my arms?

Through tear-filled eyes we study each other's face again and again. I wondered so often if I would recognize her. It has been seven years. Still, she looks like the sister I remember, only older, with serious eyes. Her hands move softly over my face. "My little sister, my little sister. I thought this day would never come."

Holding hands, we walk toward the baby's cradle. A smile lights up her face. She takes the baby in her arms, kisses his head gently. Tears flow over her cheeks. Holding the baby on one arm, she puts her other arm around me, hugging me close. "I left you a child. I find you a mother of a beautiful son.

If only all of us had lived to see this day."

"Have you heard from Mala and Yankl?" I ask anxiously.

She puts the baby gently back into the cradle, straightens his blanket slowly, sits down on the cot. I sit down next to her, my eyes glued to her face. She takes my hand in hers, sits quietly absorbed in thought.

"Have you heard from Mala and Yankl?" I ask again.

"The last time I heard from them," she says, "they were still in Poland. That was several weeks ago. Yankl and Edzia may be on their way to Germany by now. Mala, Yosef, and Abramek will take longer. It is harder to cross the border illegally with a child."

I stare at her, bewildered. "Who is Edzia? Who is Yosef? Who is Abramek? Where is Laibish, Mala's husband?"

She holds my hand tight. "I forget that you do not even know that Mala had a son. He is Abramek. He is almost six. He is a fine boy, but not very healthy. Malnutrition, poor living conditions in Russia affected his health. But he is a fine boy. A fine boy." She smiles with pride. "And Edzia is Yankl's wife."

"Yankl is married? I remember a young boy of sixteen. I cannot think of him as a married man."

She smiles. "We could not think of you as a married woman. We remember a child, and look at you. We've all changed. So much has changed." The pain returns to her eyes. She puts her arms around me as if trying to shield me from bad news. "Laibish was killed on the Russian front, fighting the Germans."

"Laibish dead! No! No!"

She holds me tight. "Abramek was only a baby. He never knew his father. Mala was a very young widow." Her voice breaks. "Yosef is her new husband. He is a good man. He is a good father to the child."

"I felt something was terribly wrong when I did not see Laibish's name on the postcard." I swallow the lump that has formed in my throat. "I tried to convince myself that it was a simple mistake, an oversight. Even when you did not mention his name in your letter, I still wanted to believe it was a mistake. I expected you all to return safely. You had escaped the Nazis. You had to return alive and well." My head spins.

"What about Uncle Baruch? His family? Aunt Balchia? Her family? They all escaped to Russia. Did you hear from them? Where are they?" My voice is high-pitched. The words rush from my mouth. "Where are they?"

Chana shakes her head. "They—they did not survive. The Nazis caught up with them when they attacked Russia. They all perished."

I bury my face in my hands and cry.

Chana puts her face close to mine. "I had to bring you more pain, my poor sister."

Chana and Moishe are permitted to share our room. We are happy to be a family again. We each delight in the baby. Pamper him. Hold him in our arms, not letting him shed a tear.

"It is good for a baby to cry a little. It is good for his lungs," a neighbor scolds.

"With four adults here to take care of his needs, he does not have to cry. His lungs will be fine. Do not worry. We have shed enough tears. This earth is flooded with our tears," I reply, annoyed.

Chana and I spend many hours talking about our childhood. About life in Poland before the war. I do not speak much about life in the ghetto. She does not ask. We are each trying to spare the other pain.

How can I tell her of all the suffering, the hunger, the fear we had to endure? How can I tell her that the day Mama was brutally taken away from us was September 10, Chana's birthday? Instead I speak of the love and devotion Motele, Laibele, Moishele, and I shared. I speak of our determination to survive. I speak of spiritual resistance. Of secret classes, secret libraries, creativity. She listens, wipes her tears, asks few questions.

I ask about life in Russia. She hesitates. "We thought that when we came home to our families we would have so much to tell. The hard years in isolated, faraway work details. Hunger, suffering." She takes a deep breath. "But when we came back we found there was no home, no family. When we learned of the horrors—" She stops again. "We were not in death camps."

We hold each other close.

One day we have wonderful news. Mala is in a Berlin displaced persons camp with her husband and son. Yankl and his wife also are in Germany in a displaced persons camp. We are all in different parts of Germany.

"At least each of us is safely out of Poland." I sigh with relief.

We hear from Mala often now. Her letters are warm, loving, full of hope. "One day we will be together again."

Mala and Yosef have asked to be transferred out of Berlin to a camp closer to us. They and Abramek are being moved to Leipheim. We, too, apply to be transferred to Leipheim. The people in the camp office assure us they will try. "We are eager to reunite families," the clerk says. "But most of the camps are already overcrowded with refugees. Do not lose hope," she adds quickly, seeing the dejection on our faces.

"As long as there is life, there is hope," I reply.

"I must remember that," she says.

twenty-two

THAT WONDERFUL DAY I have longed for, thought would never come, is here. I think I am dreaming as Chana and Moishe, Moniek, Laibele, and I step out of the truck that has brought us to the displaced persons camp in Leipheim.

I move eagerly toward the group of people waiting for the new arrivals. "Can you see her? Can you see her?" I ask Chana impatiently. I see the long, two-story brick buildings spread over a large area. "Another former concentration camp," I whisper nervously.

My heart beats faster and faster. Will I know my sister? Will she know me?

"There is Mala! There is Mala!" I hear Chana's joyful cry. She runs forward, pulling me along.

"Chanele! Rifkele!" A familiar voice reaches me.

"Mala! Mala!" I fly toward her.

We fall into each other's arms, lock in a long-awaited embrace. My eyes move, enchanted, over Mala's face. The same beautiful face, now older, filled with anguish, but still the same face that lived in my mind through all the long years of separation. I recognized her. I recognized her.

Mala moves back a little. Holds my hands tightly in hers. "Let me look at you, my dear little sister." Her voice breaks. "I was not sure I would recognize you, my own sister. . . ." She takes me in her arms again. "You have changed from the little girl I left behind in Lodz, but I knew you as soon as I saw you. The picture of you lived within my heart."

She pulls Chana toward her. The three of us hold one another, too overcome to speak.

I hear people around us sobbing. "They are lucky, so very lucky," a voice near me exclaims. "A miracle. Three sisters together again. A miracle."

A tall, skinny little boy with blue eyes and blond hair moves closer to Mala's side. He stares at me curiously. "Mommy." He tugs Mala's coat. "Mommy, is this my new aunt?"

"You are Abramek. My big six-year-old nephew." My voice quivers. I touch his face softly. "My nephew, Abramek."

"How did you know that?" He looks surprised.

"Your aunt Chana kept telling me about you, how handsome you are, how clever you are." I kiss his pale face. "Well, as soon as I saw you, I knew you must be Abramek."

He smiles shyly. "So you are my new aunt."

Tears glide down my face. "Yes, darling, yes."

I pull Moniek with the baby in his arms closer to me. If only Mama had lived to see her grandchildren. If only . . .

"Abramek, this is your new uncle, Moniek." I put Laibele's hand on Abramek's face. "And this is your Laibele, your very first cousin. He is only five months old."

His eyes wide with wonder, he touches the baby gently. "I am your cousin, Abramek. I'll take good care of you, Laibele. I am a big boy," he proclaims proudly.

Mala takes the baby in her arms. Abramek's fingers move softly over the baby's face. My heart sings. We are a family again, a family.

"I am Yosef Lubelski, your brother-in-law." Strong arms embrace me affectionately. "Riva, I feel I have known you for a very long time. Your sisters spoke of you and your little brothers. I am so happy to meet you at last." We hug like long-lost friends.

"It will be good to have everyone together. We are all going to share the same room, in block twenty-four." Like a general in charge of his little army, he leads us proudly through the camp.

The long hallway on the second floor of the building is lined with many doors. We enter a room. It is big, sunny, warm.

"That is our new home for a while." Yosef smiles, pleased.

I still think I must be dreaming. It is too good to be real. A family. A family, together at last.

twenty-three

WE SIT AROUND the table. Mala, Chana, and I hold hands. We have been together for several days now. Still we keep touching one another to reassure ourselves that it is real.

Mala's eyes are red from crying. Each time her eyes meet mine, she cries. "My little sister, had we known what horrors awaited you in Poland, we would never have let you remain there. We would have made you all come with us." She squeezes my hand. "Mama insisted that we, her older children, leave. I still hear her voice: 'You may be in danger. The Germans may take you away for forced labor. But what could happen to a widow and young children? Why would anyone harm us? I will stay here, hold on to our home, and you will have a place to return to.'"

Mala sobs. "I keep asking myself what we should have done to make her leave. We sent smugglers to bring her and the children over the Russian border to safety. Still she refused to leave. If only she had left . . ."

Mala's suffering breaks my heart.

"Mala, do not torture yourself, darling," Yosef says. "If anyone could have told us what lay ahead, would we have believed? This is the twentieth century. The Germans are a cultured people. How could anyone have grasped the horrors that a civilized people in a modern world could be capable of? How could we have believed that the Nazis were planning to annihilate our people?" His voice is filled with rage, bitterness, pain. "No, darling. We would not have believed it."

"Mama, with her strong sense of justice, of brotherhood, would never have believed it," I say. "Mala, Mama never stopped believing that the world would not be silent." I take a deep breath. "Mama's sister, Balchia, her husband, Chaim, their children, Dorka and Moniek, escaped to Russia. Her brother, Baruch, his wife, Eva, and their child, Rutka, escaped to Russia. Still they did not escape the Nazi murderers. They, too, have no graves. No, my dear sisters. Even if we had known, we would not have believed it." My voice breaks.

"I feel guilty that I survived," Mala whispers hoarsely. I look at her, astonished. "I feel guilty that I survived," she repeats. "I feel guilty that I left."

I hold her hand tightly. "I, too, feel guilty that I survived and not Mama, Motele, Laibele, Moishele. . . .

"Mala, the seven long years in Russia must have been very hard." My voice is shaky.

"Yes. But there were no death camps."

"What happened after you left Lodz? You were all trying to make your way to Bialystok, which was under Russian rule since the Russians and Germans made a nonaggression pact in 1939 and divided Poland."

She sighs. "We joined the huge flow of refugees screaming toward the new border. We did not know if or how we would make it across, but we agreed whatever happened we would try to leave messages for one another anywhere we could. We must not lose one another.

"It was a hard, dangerous journey. We reached Bialystok at different times. The city was overflowing with refugees. They slept on bare floors in schools, synagogues, in alleys. By sheer miracles, by searching for messages on synagogue walls we found one another. Yankele was with Aunt Balchia outside Bialystok, and Chanele was brought to me by Uncle Baruch. I begged Uncle Baruch to bring Yankl to me, but every move was complicated, and we were ordered to leave for labor in Siberia before we could be reunited. Again Laibish, Chana, and I left messages at the schools and synagogues about where we were being sent." She stops. Her face is twisted in pain.

"Two weeks we traveled in freight trains, spread out on the bare floors. From time to time the train stopped. Men, women, children would run quickly to relieve themselves, modesty suddenly forgotten. At the train stations they gave us hot water. Those who had money could buy little things from the small stores there."

A smile brightens her face. "I remember at one station, as the train pulled up, we saw a large group of Russians standing in line at the store. 'They are giving sugar today,' we were told by the excited Russians. Suddenly the police began to chase the people in line to buy sugar and lead us to the store.

"'Why this special treatment?' the angry Russians shouted.

"'These poor refugees come from Poland,' a policeman informed them. 'They lived in such poverty over there that they have never, never in their lives tasted sugar. We must make exceptions for these unfortunate people.'

"Riva, you must understand the Russian propaganda." Mala grins. "They make their people believe that they are better off than anyone else. And we would not dare to contradict them."

Her face is serious again. She continues. "All through the bitter journey we lamented that we did not hide in Bialystok to avoid being shipped to this faraway, forsaken place. Dressing in light clothing, we arrived in frigid Siberia. They marched us into huts, gave us cots, blankets, pillows, and told us, 'This is home now.' The next day they took us out to work, building railroad tracks. Soon we learned that people from all over Russia were sent here for hard labor.

"Each time we heard of new refugees from Poland we would rush to meet them, searching for news from Yankl. One day I met someone from Lodz. He told me that Yankl had gotten our last message in Bialystok and was trying to get to Siberia. Sometime later a transport of teenagers arrived for work. Yankl was among them. We were together again.

"From Siberia I wrote to Daddy's brother, Uncle Dovid, who lived in the Ukraine, near Kharkov, in a town called Haszkewate. I told him of the hunger, cold, hardships we could hardly endure." She sighs. "We were so unfamiliar with life in Russia and did not know that one is not permitted to complain. I could have been punished, but somehow the letter reached him and I was not arrested."

Her eyes rest on the skinny little boy playing on the floor. "My child was born in cold, icy Siberia and brought warmth into our lives. He suffered from malnutrition and was sick often. Uncle Dovid managed to get us papers for a transfer from Siberia to the

Ukraine, citing as the reason for this move the harsh Siberian climate we were not used to. On the long journey to the Ukraine, Abramek became very ill. We had to stop in the city of Kharkov to seek medical help. We knew no one there, and we had to find shelter. A kind Jewish family outside Kharkov took in Chana. Yankl we managed to get into a boys' boarding school. They sent him to work in a factory. Laibish, the baby, and I were taken in by a kind Christian family who lived in a tiny house near the railroad. They had lost their children. When we asked for help, they felt that God had sent them a family to share what little they had."

I ask Mala, "What do you mean, they had lost their children?"

"In the 1930s many people in Russia died from hunger. Some areas had it a little better than others. That family had three small children. They had no food for them. They could not stand by and see their children starve, so in desperation they put them on a train going to another region. They hoped that some kind people would have pity and take them in." Mala shakes her head. "They never found their children. They only hoped that somewhere, someone had saved their lives. They treated us as if we were their children and shared everything with us.

"We never made it to Haszkewate. We never met Uncle David. In 1941 the Germans attacked Russia. The Kharkov area was one of the first to be hit. Laibish volunteered for the Russian army to fight the Germans. I never saw him again.

"We decided that if we had to leave Kharkov we would try to get to Middle Asia. The climate was warm there, and without money, without someone to give us shelter, it would be easier to wander in a warm climate. I had gotten the address of someone in Leninabad, Middle Asia, and we agreed that if we got separated, this would be our destination.

"One night we were ordered to evacuate. Yankl was not with us. We had to leave without him. Chana, Abramek, I, and my friend Helen from Lodz, who was staying with us, left together. Helen was expecting a baby. Her husband, too, was in the Russian army." A smile brushes over Mala's face. "They found each other after the war at the address in Leninabad. That address helped reunite others, also."

"Well, we three women, one expecting, one with a baby, without money for train tickets, decided somehow to get to Middle Asia. We stole in and out of trains. On one of the trains the baby became terribly sick. I had to take him to a hospital. Chana and Helen continued toward Leninabad. As soon as the baby was better, we followed them. It took us five weeks in and out of different trains to reach Leninabad. Chana and Helen had arrived three weeks earlier.

"From Yankl we had no news. We lived in agony knowing that Kharkov, where we had left him, had fallen to the Germans. Finally we heard that the factory he worked at had been evacuated to Siberia. He was safe. And then we heard from him. He sent us money that he must have sold his rations for. Now Abramek was sick with malaria. Laibish was reported 'missing in action without a trace.'"

"You were a widow at twenty-one," I say.

She nods sadly. "For a while Yankl managed to stay in touch, and then for two years there was no word. We did not know if he was alive or dead. Chana and I worked in a factory. We were always hungry and tried to keep my sick baby alive by trading our food rations for medicine.

"One day as we tried without success to sell our last blanket to be able to buy some bread, we heard our names called. It was Yankl. He sat near a hut where they sold warm water." Her eyes well up with tears. "He could not walk. His toes were frozen and gangrene had set in. His papers and money had been stolen from him as he made his way toward Leninabad. We needed papers to get him into a hospital. In Russia you are lost without papers. We managed finally to have him admitted. His toes were amputated. When he recovered we found work for him in a town not too far from us. He worked in a gold mine."

"Why couldn't he remain with you?" I ask softly.

"We could not get permission for him to remain. He had to go where he had a job. At least he was safe and we knew where he was. I met and married Yosef in Leninabad. We were a family again and waited eagerly for the day that we would return home to find all our loved ones alive, waiting for us.

"When the Russian army liberated Poland, they gave the Polish refugees a choice of returning to Poland or remaining in Russia." She stops to catch her breath. "We wanted to go home as quickly as possible. We did not know there was no more home, no more family.

"We got into freight trains going to the Polish border. The journey was hard, but now we were going home. We reached the border at Przemysl. The train stopped. Suddenly there was shooting. Poles were shooting at the train of returning Jewish refugees!

"Abramek fell off the train at the station and was hurt. We rushed him to the hospital. Yankl and I remained in the hospital with him. Yosef and Chana could not remain. They continued with the transport. We agreed to meet in Lodz. Abramek was still sick when we had to leave the hospital. Gangs of the Polisk A.K. searched the hospital for Jews. The ones they found, they dragged out and murdered. We barely escaped with our lives.

"Some people we ran into told us that the transport Yosef and Chana were with was sent to Upper Szlezia. At that time you could go only where the train was going, not where you wanted to go. So, by moving from one train to another, we, too, made our way to Upper Szlezia. Wherever we stopped, we would go to the Jewish Committee and the marketplace. Those were the places people searched for family, for friends. There we learned that Yosef and Chana had gone to Lodz. There, also, we heard the good news that you had survived and were in Lodz. We searched for a way to get onto a train going to Lodz.

"It was dangerous for a Jew to be on a Polish train. We found a friend who was an officer in the Polish army. The military had a better chance to get onto a train. Abramek and I posed as his wife and child and traveled in the railroad car for high-ranking military personnel. Yankl could not be with us, but our friend put a military cap on Yankl and got him into the next railroad car.

"At one of the stations where the train

had stopped, the A.K. gang removed all the Jews they could find. Our friend brought Yankl to our railroad car because the A.K. did not search the railroad car of the high-ranking military. He helped us reach Lodz safely. We found Yosef and Chana but no one else from our family. You had already left Poland for the displaced persons camp in Germany.

"We shared an apartment with friends — eleven in two rooms — as we searched for ways to leave the cursed Polish earth that was again soaking up Jewish blood. Once we learned that you were in Pocking, we had a new place to meet if we became separated. Again we had to part. Again we had to search for safety. Yankl and Edzia and Chana and Moishe, who had married in Lodz, made their way to Germany with a group of young people. That group, led by the Jewish Agency for Palestine, was bringing Jews over the border to Austria and Germany. Yosef, Abramek, and I were smuggled across the border. And now, at last, we are together again — after seven lost years."

My thoughts wander. Seven lost years . . .

I hear the baby cry and look around startled. Abramek holds the baby in his arms.

I gasp. "Please be careful, Abramek. He is only a baby." I move quickly to his side and support the baby with my hands.

"Don't worry, Auntie. I won't hurt the baby." He smiles confidently as he puts the baby back into the carriage. "I'm a big boy. His big cousin." His voice is filled with pride. "I didn't want the baby to cry."

I hug him. "Yes, darling. You are his big cousin and my big helper."

I bend down to pull up his knee socks. "We have to fatten you up a bit, my helper. Your socks cannot stay up on your bony legs."

"I'm getting strong, Auntie. Here, feel my muscles." He flexes his skinny arms proudly.

"My, my, you do have muscles. Now, my sweet muscle man, you may wheel the carriage slowly back and forth to help your cousin fall asleep."

All eyes are on him as he moves the carriage slowly back and forth, humming softly. Someone makes a sound. He puts his finger to his lips, then points to the baby.

I look at Mala and Chana. We all have tears in our eyes.

We have a new generation. We are building a new tomorrow. Maybe it will be the tomorrow of justice and brotherhood Mama so strongly believed in.

twenty-four

I MARVEL AT the cultural activities that blossom in the displaced persons camp. The hunger for learning that kept our spirits alive in the ghetto and death camps survived.

There are few children here. My heart goes out to the little survivors. They lived in underground bunkers, in Christian homes as Christian children, or they were born in Russia. They suffered constant fear of being caught, betrayed, killed. They are subdued, shy, but eager to learn.

I look at the pale, solemn faces, the bewildered eyes and see again the children of the ghetto. I hear again the voice of my former kindergarten teacher, Mrs. Muster, who risked her life to keep up a kindergarten in the ghetto.

Riva, I need your help. We have no teachers. You are a product of this kindergarten, of the Jewish day school, the Medem Shul. You must help me. The children here need us. We have to stand by them as long as we can. If we bring a smile to their faces, even for a moment . . .

I see again her tear-stained face. *Riva, each minute that we survive, we defeat our enemies. We must make each minute count.*

She did not survive. The children did not survive. They perished at the hands of the Nazis. I see their defiant spirit, their hunger for life in the eyes of the children here.

Mrs. Perlow, a warm, sensitive educator with a keen understanding of the needs of these children, organizes a school. I sit across from her, telling her about Mrs. Muster, "her" children, her courage. "Mrs. Perlow, the children here need to smile again. I want to help."

"Your teacher—had she survived— would have been very happy, Riva. She left you her legacy: caring. I would be happy to have your help."

I sit on the floor, five solemn children encircling me. Their eyes hang on my face. I smile. Their expressions remain the same— serious, sad. "Who wants to learn a Yiddish song?" I ask cheerfully, trying to conceal the pain within me. No answer.

"Come on," I coax. "I know you all want to learn this song. It's easy. Just repeat after me.

"A little boy, a little girl,
A little girl, a little boy,
Let's both dance,
Let's all rejoice,
Let's all dance."

Softly they repeat the words after me.

"Louder, children. Louder. Let me hear your voices."

A little girl of five raises her hand timidly. "Teacher, is it all right to raise our voices?" she whispers.

I take her into my arms. Hold her tight. "Yes, darling, yes. Let's raise our voices as loudly as we can, children, as loudly as we can."

Slowly, cautiously, their voices gain strength. But their eyes throw fearful glances at the door, at the window. Will they ever stop living in fear?

"Wonderful! Wonderful! Children, take one another's hands. Let's dance."

We form a circle. "Sway to the left. Sway to the right. Stomp your feet." They sway and stomp their feet.

"Now let's sing as we dance.

"I am a Jewish child,

I sing a Yiddish song.

I am. I am. I am.

I am a Jewish child."

Voices get stronger. Feet move faster. They sing. They dance. They fall to the floor, worn out, making happy sounds. Tears glide over my face.

Each time we are together I rejoice in their eagerness to learn a new song, a new poem, a new game. They are more relaxed. They smile more often. There are few older children. Mrs. Perlow works with them. They thrive. I read stories to the little ones, recall fairy tales from my childhood. They sit, silent and wide-eyed, as Cinderella is found by the prince.

"And they lived happily ever after," they repeat after me.

They listen, enchanted, as I sing the songs from the play *Cinderella*, which I saw with my classmates when I was ten years old. The songs tell of courage, of hope, and teach to believe that good must win over evil.

"Do the bad people go away forever after, teacher?" A little boy lifts his brown curly head.

They all stare at me now. They wait for my answer. They must have an answer. What do I say? What do I tell them? They need to feel safe.

"Will they come back again, the bad people?" two dark eyes demand to know.

I compose myself. "We will not let them come back." My voice is strong.

"We will not let them come back," one child repeats defiantly.

I hear a sigh of relief.

Yosef, my brother-in-law, used to perform on the Yiddish stage in Poland when Jewish life, Jewish culture were in full bloom.

"We must lift the spirits of the survivors by bringing back to them the world that we lost through Yiddish theater. Through plays and songs from our past, we will draw the strength to build a future." He is filled with excitement.

A theater group forms under his direction. Mala, too, joins the group. They travel to the many displaced persons camps in Germany, bringing Yiddish plays and concerts to them.

Yosef is thrilled. "Riva, I wish you could see how eagerly they wait for our arrival. They greet us like old friends. We bring them the voices of the past, the good and the evil. We remind them that we, the remnants of our people, must carry on." He clears his throat. "It is up to us to rise from the ashes and build a new life."

I am filled with awe as I watch him on the stage in Leipheim. The people around me cry and laugh. Shout their anger. Burst into song as they wander with him from yesterday to today, to tomorrow.

I watch Mala, dressed in black and sitting on the darkened stage amid rubble. I know it is my sister, but on that stage she is every one of us who returned to the ruins of our homes, found rubble or strangers where our families once lived. Her pain-filled voice is the voice of all who survived and found only ashes. Her mournful lament fills the theater.

"Where is my street?

Where is my home?

Where is my family so dear to me?

There is no more street.

There is no more home.

Perished the family that I loved so much."

Her voice filled with everyone's anger, everyone's pain, she wails:

"Where are the children who sang and danced here?

Where did they all disappear to?"

Her voice becomes a hoarse whisper.

"Murdered, murdered in front of their mothers."

Her voice takes on a sudden strength.

"The day of vengeance for the spilled blood must come,

for each ruined life,

for each home,

for each street."

She stops, looks around.

"The day of reckoning is here . . .

but . . .

the score, the score . . .

The score is too big."

She cries bitterly. We all cry with her. The score is too big.

twenty-five

THE CROWDED DISPLACED persons camps are under the supervision of the United Nations Relief and Rehabilitation Administration, or UNRRA. The camp is administered by different camp committees. The members of the committees are survivors who live in the camp.

The food that is rationed to the displaced persons is supplied by UNRRA or the American Jewish Joint Committee, or JOINT, and other international relief organizations. Food previously unfamiliar to us—canned meats, condensed milk, powdered eggs—become part of our daily diet. The children receive some fresh milk, fresh eggs, extra rations, and sometimes cocoa.

We are given the choice of using our ration cards to eat in the community dining hall or taking the allocated food to do our own cooking on the little stoves in our rooms. No matter which we choose, there are always long, slow-moving lines. Our gloomy days are spent mostly in these lines that bring back vivid, painful memories of the ghetto. Mala and Chana, too, remember the food lines in Russia and always wonder if there will be enough for all the people in line.

I stare at the somber, haggard faces of the survivors waiting patiently in line for food and keep reminding myself that I am free. This is not a ghetto. This is not a concentration camp. I am free.

Mala, Chana, and I choose to use our food rations for cooking. Warm aromas of cooked meals fill the room, giving it the feeling of home. Each simple meal is a feast. We are together. We are a family.

I make chocolate pudding from flour, condensed milk, and cocoa for the children.

"I wish I, too, were a child." Yosef grins. "And I, too, would get to eat chocolate pudding."

Abramek moves closer to Yosef. "I'll share with you, Daddy."

Yosef smiles, pleased with the child's generosity. "Thank you, son. I was only teasing. I'm glad that we have pudding for you and Laibele." He hugs Abramek. "My mother made chocolate pudding when I was a child. The kitchen smelled so good. She would let me scrape the pot and lick the spoon."

I swallow the lump in my throat and move the empty pot toward Yosef and Abramek. "Look, that pot, too, needs scraping. Be a child again, Yosef. Show us how to do it."

"All right, I'll show you." He takes the child onto his lap as if to teach him a very important skill. A warm smile brightens his face. Eagerly, joyfully, father and son scrape the pot and lick the spoon.

Relief organizations collect new and used clothing for the displaced people in the camps. The clothing is entrusted to the clothing committee for distribution. Often the clothing that arrives is useless to us, who spend our days standing in lines for one thing or another. It consists of evening gowns, dressy shoes, old suits, hats.

I feel like a beggar waiting for a handout as I stand in line for shoes and sweaters.

Yosef, who is on the clothing committee, unpacks a new shipment of shoes. The sizes are either very big or very small, nothing that we can use. He opens a crate with many dresses. He looks frustrated. The crate is filled with fancy dresses. The people standing idly in line stare at him blankly.

"Don't worry, friends," Yosef announces. There is defiance in his voice. "I will find a use for these clothes."

"Are we having a masquerade ball?" someone asks sarcastically.

Yosef grins. "No, friend, but we have a theater here. I will use some of the clothes for theater costumes." There is a twinkle in his eyes. "I am planning a skit in which a partisan woman has to pose as a dance-hall girl. Her mission is to get close and kill a vicious Nazi officer who is responsible for the death of Jewish men, women, and children." He pulls a shimmering black satin dress from the crate, examines it carefully. "This will be perfect for a dance-hall girl." A triumphant smile lights up his eyes.

Some stare at him silently. Others shake their heads.

"The ideas this man comes up with," someone mumbles in admiration.

"He makes the best of every situation," someone else says.

The talk in the line now turns to our uncertain future.

"When will all this end?"

"How long will we stand in lines for food, for clothing, for a chance to leave this place, this land?"

"How long? How long?"

Bitter, dejected voices ask the same questions again and again.

twenty-six

A NEW SPARK of life is brought to the camp by the Organization for Rehabilitation through Training (ORT). Their workshops to train and retrain the survivors in work skills and make them independent are well attended. I join a class in knitting gloves. It feels good to learn a new skill. It feels good to be alive.

We sit in a circle, a group of nine women. We are bound by the same eagerness to be useful, to be productive. Someone sings an old Yiddish song.

"I am a happy, carefree fellow.

Tra-la-la. Tra-la-la.

I wander to all corners of the world."

The song brings back memories. My friends and I sang this happy tune as we wandered carefree from one activity to another: school, clubs, libraries. How different the song sounds now. But the bouncy, happy tune survived. I still wander from place to place, but I am not free to choose my destination.

"I wander to all corners of the world," the young woman sings softly.

"Is there a corner of the world for us?" another woman asks bitterly. The woman stops her singing.

"Is there a place for us?"

"Where do we go from here?" others echo.

"Only a few countries have opened their doors to the survivors of the death camps. And the restrictions eliminate most of us." Mrs. Usherowicz, the oldest of the little group, sighs painfully. "I am one of the lucky ones, one of the very few with a husband and grown son. We faced death, still managed to stay together, remain a family. Now they want to separate us." She wipes her eyes. "The countries that may let in my son do not want us. Wrong trade, too old . . . My husband and I are only in our forties." She sits still for a while, the knitting in her lap. "The only place for us is the land of Israel—if we can make it there safely." Her voice is determined, defiant. "They will not separate us. Whatever we face, we will face together."

"We survived and still live in fear of tomorrow," another woman says. "In the concentration camps we believed that when the day of freedom finally came, the world would reach out to us with compassion, eager to help us."

"The world did not care then, the world does not care now," someone else replies.

I hear the anger, the bitterness in the women's voices. I feel the same anger, the same bitterness. I think of Mama's words. *A world full of people will not be silent.*

I rush back to my room, take my child in my arms, and hug him tight. The gloom, the helplessness vanish. Pain, uncertainty, fear give way to rays of hope. There must be some people who care. . . .

Packages of food and clothing come from our relatives in Argentina. Their letters are full of love and concern. They are trying to bring us to Argentina, but our chances are very, very slim: rules, regulations, quotas.

Mala, Chana, and I do not speak of it, but deep in our hearts lies the fear of new separation. It is written on our faces. Not again. Not again.

My brother Yankl writes: "Canada needs tailors. I know how to sew. I may have a chance to leave the displaced persons camp in Schweibishal." Tears fill my eyes. We had so little time together when we met shortly after we came to Leipheim. Now separation again. Maybe forever.

Separation. Separation. Separation. The word hammers in my head. But what choice do we have? We cannot remain in Germany. If one of us has a chance to leave, to build a new life, we must let him go. Logic dictates: Let them go. But my heart does not understand logic. It cries.

I search eagerly for a sponsor to help us leave — and live in fear of that day. Will I be able to face separation again? Will I have the strength to say good-bye again?

twenty-seven

"DARLING! DARLING!" MONIEK calls, excited. His face flushed, he stands in the doorway holding a letter. "From America."

"From America? It has been a long time since we heard from Froiem Zelmanowicz."

"No, darling. It is not from Zelmanowicz. But I think we can thank him for it." His voice quivers. "It is from Morris Borenstein. Etta Borenstein was my mother's sister."

"A letter from your family! Open it, darling, open it."

He remains standing with the envelope clenched in his hands. "You open it, Riva." He hands me the envelope.

I read the return address. Morris Borenstein, 16 Clark Street, Malden, Mass., U.S.A. I tear open the envelope and read:

My dear nephew Moishe,

My name is Moishe, too. Moishe Borenstein. I am the husband of your mother's sister, Etta. It pains me to tell you that your aunt Etta passed away. It breaks my heart that she did not live to see the day she waited for: the day someone from the family she left behind in Poland would write and say I am alive, I survived.

Your cousins and I are so very happy to hear from you. Are there any other survivors in our family?

I come from the same region as your parents, Chava and Laibl. We grew up together. When Etta and I left Poland a long time ago, we urged your parents to leave, also. They did not want to part with the family. Had they left . . .

Life is so strange. It is amazing how we found you. I received a phone call from a member of the men's club I belong to. He asked if I knew anybody by the name of Senderowicz from Wyszogrod, Poland. My heart stopped. I said my late wife's sister's married name was Senderowicz. They lived in Wyszogrod, Poland, and we had not heard from them since the Nazis occupied Poland.

He said he had news, good news. In the Jewish Daily Forward he had read a list of Holocaust survivors searching for relatives in America. One of them, a Moishe Senderowicz, was searching for a family named Borenstein in the Boston area. "Moishe," he asked, "could this be your family? I felt I must call you and ask, just in case you knew the name Senderowicz, or the Borenstein he is looking for."

My head was spinning as the people at the newspaper gave me your address. I thought I was dreaming. After all the years of not knowing, finally, finally we had heard from someone. I had given up. If only my dear Etta had lived to see that day. My children and I are eager to help in any way we can. Please let us know what we can do. We will get in touch with HIAS and find out how we can bring you to America. Our hearts are full of joy.

Be well. Be strong.
Your Uncle Moishe

Tears flow over my face. I put my arms around Moniek and hold him tight. His face, too, is wet. "I have family," he whispers. "There is someone in this world who knew my parents, my grandparents. I wonder sometimes if I ever had parents, grandparents, brothers. I just found my ties to the past."

He reaches for paper and pen. His hands are shaking. "Please, Riva, you write, I'll dictate. I cannot hold the pen in my hands."

I take the pen from his trembling hands and write.

Dear Uncle Moishe,

I have no words to describe how I felt when I received your letter. I still do not believe that I have found family.

It is two years since I was liberated from the Nazi death camps. I went back home to Wyszogrod, the place of my birth, the place where I last saw my family alive. But there was no one left. My parents, my brothers, Shmuel

Nussen and Berl, all my aunts, uncles, cousins. A large family, but they just vanished. I keep on searching. I try to convince myself that since I survived, why not someone else? Maybe they are alive, and I will find them if I keep on searching. I must keep on believing in miracles. My survival was a miracle. Every day for six years I faced death, and still I am here. I must not stop seaching. I must not stop hoping.

I am married now. Her name is Riva. She, too, is a Holocaust survivor. We are building a new life together. We have a beautiful little boy. We named him Laibl, after my father. My father's name lives on.

I am sorry to hear that Aunt Etta passed away. I wish I had known her. My mother spoke of her often. Please send me pictures of each one of you so I can meet you through pictures until the lucky day comes that we all meet in person. I will send you pictures of us.

Please, if you have pictures of my parents, brothers, please, please send them to me. I do not have a single picture of my family. Everything is gone. I try to recall what they looked like, but their faces are all blurred.

I hope we will meet you soon. It is strange, it is wonderful to know that somewhere in a far-away land, a family I never met is waiting for me, eager to help. I thank you with all my heart.

I am happy that you are contacting HIAS. They will tell you how to sponsor us and help us leave Germany. I know it is very complicated to bring people from the displaced persons camps to America. But at least now we have a chance. I do not feel alone anymore. Give my love to all my cousins.

Your nephew,
Moishe Senderowicz

He looks drained. I hold him close. "As long as there is life," I whisper softly.

We have more happy news, this time from my brother Yankl. His wife, Edzia, gave birth to a little girl May 13, 1947, in the displaced persons camp in Schweibishal, Germany. They named their daughter Nacha, after Mama. They still hope to emigrate to Canada.

And on July 5, 1947, my sister Chana has a son. They name him Shiele, after my brother-in-law's father. Another name passed on.

Chana is in a German hospital in Ginsburg. The displaced persons camp in Leipheim has only a clinic. I go to see her and meet my new nephew.

It is still difficult for me to walk through the German streets, visit a German hospital. But Chana's room is bright and cheerful. Her face is aglow as she cuddles her son. I take the baby in my arms, hold him close. Yes, yes, as long as there is life . . .

twenty-eight

THE DISPLACED PERSONS camp has its own police force. Moniek and my brother-in-law Moishe join the police force. Work makes them feel useful, keeps them busy. The police station is located in block six, at the entrance to the camp. It is a long, one-story building with the police station on the ground floor. The second floor houses the policemen and their families, for the police personnel must live near the station.

We are assigned our own room. I look around the tiny room with its slanted roof and small window and I feel alone, closed in again. I run to Chana's room a few doors away to assure myself that I am not alone, that I still have family nearby. I wonder what will happen when the day comes that we must leave for America. Will I be able to leave my sisters again? I wait for that day. I fear that day.

Laibele's smile brings sunshine into my troubled heart, chasing the gloom. I marvel at the power of a child's smile. He is a happy, healthy child, the joy of our lives. He is already one year old. We celebrate his first birthday with family and friends. The little room emptied of the beds is now filled with people for our very first party.

"What did you do to this room, Riva?" asks a friend. "The tiny room has been stretched for this happy occasion. Look at all the people it holds."

"Like the Red Sea that parted for the Jews to go to freedom, these walls parted for the survivors to rejoice in life," I reply, my face flushed. "A new Jewish child, our child, is one year old today."

Someone begins to sing. There is laughter, there is joy around me. Many voices, jubilant voices, fill the room.

"Who would ever believe that we would sing, laugh again," someone remarks.

"Who would ever believe that we would live to celebrate the birthdays of a new generation." Another voice is heard.

"We were not supposed to survive, but look at us. We are here."

"We celebrate the birthday of a Jewish child in the land of our murderers."

"Hitler must be turning over in his grave."

"Never say this is the final road for you," someone sings. That song, written in the ghetto of Vilno by Hirsh Glick, became the anthem of the underground resistance movement. Later it spread to other ghettos and to the Jewish partisans fighting the

Nazis in the woods of Poland. We all join in.
"Never say this is the final road for you,
Though leaden skies cover over days
    of blue.
As the hour that we longed for is so
    near,
Our step beats out the message, we
    are here.
From lands so green with palms to
    lands all white with snow,
We shall be coming with our anguish
    and our woe.
And where a spurt of our blood fell on
    the earth,
There our courage and our spirit have
    rebirth.
The early morning sun will brighten
    our day,
And yesterday with our foe will fade
    away.
But if the sun delays and in the east
    remains,
This song as password generations
    must maintain.
This song is written with our blood
    and not with lead,
It's not a little tune that birds sing
    overhead.
This song a people sang amid collapsing
    walls.
With grenades in hand they heeded
    the call.

Therefore never say the road now
   ends for you,
Though leaden skies may cover days
   of blue.
As the hour that we longed for is so
   near,
Our steps beat out the message, we
   are here!"

The words dance before me. We had the
courage, the strength to survive. We must
have the courage, the strength to rebuild.
We have a new generation.

"L'chaim! To life! To our new generation!" Someone raises a glass of wine.

"L'chaim! To life! To our children!" we
echo.

twenty-nine

THE DAY IS warm and sunny. I sit on a bench in front of block six, watching my little boy play on the grass. People walk by, some engaged in heated discussions, some silent, somber. I study their faces and wonder what they are thinking, what they are feeling. Are they living in the past, the present, or dreaming of the future? Most of the survivors are in their twenties and thirties. Very seldom is there an older person or a teenager. Most of the children here were born after the Holocaust.

A young woman pushing a baby in a carriage sits down next to me. She places the carriage close to her side. She turns toward me. "Do you mind if I sit here?" she whispers, not to wake the sleeping baby.

"I appreciate the company," I whisper back.

She mumbles something as she wheels the carriage slowly back and forth.

"How old is your baby?" I ask softly.

Her eyes glow as she looks toward the baby. "My little girl is six months old." She fixes the baby's blanket carefully. "I do not know what I would do without her."

"I know how you feel." My eyes are on my child. "I wonder if other mothers are so attached to their children, too. Are we over-protective?"

She does not answer, absorbed in thoughts of her own.

"I live in constant fear of losing my baby," she says suddenly. "Tell me this is normal." She holds on tightly to the carriage, as if someone were lurking nearby to snatch her baby from her.

"Who can say what is normal for us? Or if we are normal. I often wonder how we still manage to go on as we do."

"We should all be running around mad." Her voice is low, distant. "We should be running around mad."

We sit silently, watching our children. I glance at the young woman. She seems to be in another world. Her hands twitch nervously. Her lips move silently.

Maybe we are mad, I think as I watch her face twisted in pain.

The baby in the carriage stirs, cries out in her sleep. The mother grabs her quickly, holds her tight, pressing the baby's face into her sweater. Her eyes wild, she whispers frantically, "Quiet. Quiet. Do not cry, my child. Do not cry." Sweat is dripping from her face.

I stare at her, bewildered. "What is wrong with you? Let the baby breathe." I pull the sweater off the baby's face. "What is wrong with you?"

She stares at me as if trying to remember where she is. "Oh, my God. Oh, my God." She cradles the child in her arms, crying hysterically. "My poor baby. Did I hurt you? Did I hurt you?"

"The baby is fine. Calm down, please, calm down." I touch her arm lightly. She pulls back.

"Your baby is fine," I stammer, confused.

She wipes her face, turns toward me. "I am sorry. I have to explain. You must think I am crazy." She caresses the baby's hair with shaking hands. "I have to explain." She sobs. "I survived hidden in a bunker, a hole in the ground on a Polish farm. We were nine people there. Seven adults and two small children. We lived in silence. If we had been discovered, the Nazis would have killed us and the Polish farmer with his family."

She takes a deep breath. "But how do you keep small children quiet all the time? The children, too, must have felt that they must be quiet. I do not know how. They were so little. But they were silent most of the time. If a child cried, the motehr would quickly cover the child's face with a pillow to muffle the sound. When I heard the baby cry, I forgot where we are. Suddenly I was one of the mothers in the bunker and had to silence my crying baby." She closes her eyes. "One of the children suffocated." Her voice is hollow. "The mother lost the will to live any longer. She died."

I gasp. She, too, almost suffocated her baby.

"I am still in the bunker. Even here," she mumbles.

We sit silently, each lost in the past. My heart cries for the mother who lost her child. For the child who lost its life. For the woman next to me who still lives in the bunker.

I reach out for my child. Hold him close. *We should be running around mad* rings in my ears.

thirty

LISTS, LISTS, LISTS. They are forever tied to our existence. Forever part of our lives.

In the ghetto the constant fear of finding one's name on a list for deportation hung threateningly over us. After liberation we searched eagerly the lists of known survivors posted on walls of Jewish relief organizations, only to walk away heartbroken. Now our names are on lists for strange-sounding countries, faraway places that we hope will open their doors for those who survived the Nazi death camps.

My brother, his wife, and child have left for Canada. He placed his name on a list of tailors. He was picked. I am happy he is out of Germany. But will I ever see him again?

Moniek and I are still waiting to hear what our chances are of going to America. We hear often from our family there. They send packages, money, letters of moral support. But obtaining visas is a very long, slow process.

Again we check the lists, hoping to find our names.

Under Yosef's direction, the theater brightens our lives with new plays, concerts. We laugh, cry, dream of a place that we can call home. The children in our school and kindergarten blossom like flowers. But the fear of tomorrow, the uncertainty hovers over us, lies heavy in our minds. Even in the minds of our children at play.

"Will you go to America if they let you go?" I hear one ask another.

"That is a silly question," comes an annoyed reply. "There is no one there that wants us. How can I go to America?"

The other children shake their heads in agreement.

"My parents put their names on a list for a country called Venezuela," one child declares, struggling with the name.

"Where is Venu—Venu—or whatever the name is?" another asks curiously.

"My mother said it is at the other end of the world."

"Where is the other end of the world?"

"I do not know." The child shrugs his shoulders. "Somewhere over tall, tall mountains and deep, deep oceans . . . I think."

They sit quietly, absorbed in thoughts.

"There is a Jewish land, my parents say," one child announces, breaking the silence. "They want to go there. But they say it is too dangerous for me. There is war over there."

"You mean they are killing people?" comes a frightened question.

"They are always killing people in war, don't you know?" The boy whose parents want to go to Israel stands up, stretches out to the full height of his six-year-old frame. "But I am not afraid. I am big and strong. I can fight." He throws punches in the air, fighting an invisible enemy.

Their talk brings me back to the children of the ghetto again. They, too, were ready to fight for the right to live. I remember their talks, their games: fighting the Nazis; hiding from the Nazis; escaping to a land where they would be free.

Is there such a land for our children? Will our children ever live normal lives?

In the kindergarten a little girl says, "Teacher, remember the poem we learned of the little sailboat that travels over oceans? Why can't we take a sailboat, go far, far away to anyplace we want to?"

"Why can't we? Why can't we?" others echo.

They all stare at me, waiting for an answer. A teacher must have all the answers. . . .

"Because we need permission."

"Who do we need permission from?"

"From the countries we would want to live in."

"If we are very, very good, will they give us permission?"

My eyes well up with tears. I wipe them quickly.

"Do not cry, teacher." A little boy with dark, curly hair falling over his eyes takes my hand. "We will be very, very good."

"Yes, we will be very, very quiet."

"We know how to be very, very quiet."

"Will they give us permission if we promise to be good?"

"Someday someone will give us permission," I tell the children. "Someday we will go on big, big ships over wide, deep oceans, like our little sailboat—and find a new home."

"Can we go on a plane, teacher?"

"Maybe."

"Can we go on a train, teacher? I have never, never been on a train."

"Someday we will do all those things." I, too, become excited. "Someday we will do all those things. Just wait and see."

"But"—a little girl with a red ribbon in her hair tugs my sleeve—"will we still be together? I do not want to leave my friends."

There is a sudden silence. "Maybe someday we will all meet again."

"Maybe. Maybe." I hear a sigh.

thirty-one

SLOWLY PASS DAYS, years fly by fast. A poem I learned as a child keeps spinning in my head.

The days drag very, very slowly, as we wait for some news on our chances to emigrate from the displaced persons camp in Germany to a land that will give us a home. Days turn into months, months into years. It is 1948. Three years after liberation from the Nazi concentration camps, we are still here, in Germany, in a former concentration camp.

A new child is born into our family. Mala has a little girl on June 5, 1948. They name her Esther, after Yosef's mother. "Another name passed on," I whisper softly, holding the new member of our family in my arms. "Another name passed on."

Our son, Laibele, is two years old. I teach him Yiddish poems, Yiddish songs. He learns eagerly. Proudly he recites the poems to his aunts, uncles, cousins, his family. I listen to the happy voices of the children, our new generation, and feel overwhelmed by the miracle before me. If only we could remain a family. If only we could remain together.

If we put our names on the same lists, maybe we will all emigrate together. There is a list for Bolivia, South America, a land we know nothing about. But if it keeps us together . . . We put our names on that list and live in fear. What if they grant a visa to one and not to the others?

I know others envy us, and rightly so. We are three sisters who survived. We are a family. But after seven years of separation we live in constant fear of being torn apart again.

We are all rejected. Wrong trades. I sigh with relief. We still have some time together. . . .

It may take years for Moniek, Laibele, and me to get visas for America, if we should ever get them. There are quotas, rules, regulations. I am not sure if I should be happy or sad.

New people arrive. Others depart, some to other camps. Some to other countries. We bid them good-bye, wish them luck.

"Do not forget my name if you should meet someone."

The message is always the same. The questions of the new arrivals are always the same.

"What is your name?"

"Where are you from?"

"Did you ever hear my name . . . any-where?"

"What camps were you in?"

"Were you in hiding?"

"Were you in Russia?"

"Did you find family?"

"We will never stop searching," someone remarks.

"We will always live with false hope," says another.

"If the ones who perished had graves, maybe it would help to accept the terrible truth that they are dead. If only they had graves," a woman says.

"If, if, if!" a man shouts, his eyes flashing with anger. "Always if. We will search forever. We will live forever in pain and agony. I envy the dead. They do not have to suffer any longer."

"Don't speak that way!" a woman shouts. "It is a sin. We are alive. We must go on living. We must live with hope. Only the dead are without hope."

"We are living dead," the man argues. "What did we survive for? To suffer more."

A man in his forties, with deep, sad eyes, moves toward him. "The woman here is right. Only the dead are without hope." His voice is low, slow, deliberate. "We who survived have a mission."

"A mission to live in agony?"

"To bear witness. To remember." His words are strong, clear.

"I do not want to remember! I remember too much! I want to forget!" shouts the angry man.

They stare at each other silently.

"We must remember. We must remember." The words sound like a command.

"We must remember," others echo.

"We must remember our children, their agonizing screams, their last breaths."

"We must remember those who perished with God's name on their lips."

"We must remember the outcries of vengeance."

"We must remember our dead, their hopes, dreams."

"We are bound forever by the flames of the crematoriums."

"We must always remember."

"We must tell the world."

"We must tell our children."

"I will protect my children from that pain." An angry voice rises above the others. "I will keep silent. Our children must have normal lives. I will protect them from our agony. I will keep our pain to myself."

"Someday your children will ask why they have no grandparents, aunts, uncles. How will you answer?"

There is deadly silence.

How will you answer? echoes in my ears. *How will you answer?*

thirty-two

I RECEIVE A letter from my friend Karola. It has been over two years since we said a hasty good-bye in Wroclaw. Together we shared the horrors of the ghetto, camps, the journey back home. Then we had to part. Now we have found each other again. She is in a displaced persons camp in Berlin with Oscar and their son, Mendel. They are out of Poland. I am overjoyed.

I write to her immediately.

Dear Karola and Oscar,

We are so happy finally to hear from you. I have many questions, but the most important one is: Was it Moniek's brother who asked about him in Wroclaw after we left? Someone in the Berlin displaced persons camp told Moniek that a man who could have been his brother Shmuel came to the apartment we had once shared and asked about him. Did you see this man? We have been searching for a trace of him ever since, to no avail. Did you see him? Did you speak to him? Was it Moniek's brother?

We are well. We are waiting eagerly for your answer.

Love, Riva

Moniek is full of hope again. "It was Shmuel. It was Shmuel. Karola and Oscar must have spoken to him. We'll find him. You will see. My brothers were young. They were still healthy last time I saw them. I survived. They must be alive somewhere. I am sure it was Shmuel who was looking for me."

I watch Moniek being carried away on wings of hope. I, too, am filled with hope. Yet a small, nagging voice whispers in my ear. Why did Karola not say anything about Moniek's brother in her letter? She wrote about Oscar, the baby, friends, but didn't say anything about Moniek's brother having been there. Why not? Did she assume that they had found each other? She would have expressed her joy. It is not often that we have reason to rejoice. Maybe, whispers the ugly little voice, it is all a mistake. It happens so often. Maybe it was not Moniek's brother. Maybe it was a stranger looking for someone else.

I do not voice my thoughts. I wonder silently if Moniek has the same thoughts. I watch him lie awake at night, stare at the darkness. Is there darkness within him, too?

"Are you all right?" I ask softly.

He does not answer. I put my arm

around him. "Are you thinking of your brothers?"

He puts his head on my chest silently. We hold each other close.

"Soon we will hear from Karola. It will be good news," I whisper. "Soon we will hear from Karola."

My hands tremble as I hold Karola's long-awaited letter. Moniek is not at home.

Dear Riva,

We were so happy finally to find you again. I keep on staring at the picture of your son. I am so happy for you and Moniek.

I am surprised by your strange question. Did we see Moniek's brother in Wroclaw? We do not know of anyone who asked for you or Moniek while we were in Wroclaw. But maybe we were not at home. You know that people in transit, searching for families, often stayed in our apartment. It is possible that someone did ask for Moniek. Everything is possible. We still believe in miracles. I wish I could confirm this miracle, say yes, I met Moniek's brother and he is alive and well. Tell Moniek not to give up.

What are your future plans? As if we have anything to do with our future plans . . . We are trying to go to America, God willing. Oscar has family there. Maybe someday we will meet again. We shared so much pain, it would be good to share some joy.

❋ ❋ ❋

I swallow my tears. How do I tell Moniek? The dream we dared to dream of Karola confirming that his brother is alive just turned to ashes again. How do I tell Moniek?

My heart pounds as he enters the tiny room. I wish I had somewhere to hide. I avoid looking at him, afraid my face will betray me.

He picks up our son, holds him high in the air. The child laughs with delight. "You are getting bigger every day, Laibele." He hugs him and puts him down again.

Moniek turns to hug me. "Any mail today, sweetheart?" His voice is anxious, impatient.

"Yes, there is." My voice trembles.

"Is it from Karola?"

"Yes." I swallow hard. "It is from Karola."

"Well? Did she see Shmuel? What did he look like? What did he say?" Excited questions race from his mouth.

Silently I hand him the letter. He studies my face with horror and sits down heavily on the cot. He reads the letter slowly. The letter falls from his hands to the floor. He sits motionless. I put my arms around him. He sobs. I sob.

"Moniek." I search for words of comfort. "Moniek, Karola said that someone *might* have looked for you in Wroclaw. Just because she did not meet him . . . You know how people come and go now. One could have been Shmuel. We cannot give up. We must not give up."

Tears fall over Moniek's face. Laibele stares at him. "Why are you crying, Daddy?"

Moniek wipes his eyes quickly. He takes Laibele in his arms.

"I am not crying, son. See, I am not crying."

He turns toward me. "We live with the horrors of the past. We hold on to false hopes. But we live. Life goes on."

thirty-three

I AM EXPECTING a second child. A new life is growing inside of me. It makes my heart sing with joy.

Moniek holds my hand tenderly. His face is radiant. "A little brother or sister for Laibele. Another name will come to life again."

I move closer to him. "Before Laibele was born, we hoped that our child would be born in America, the land of freedom. More than two years later, we are still here. The land of freedom is still only a dream." I sigh. "Maybe this child will be born in America. I wish. I hope."

"No matter where our child is born—I, too, wish it to be America—it will bring joy into our lives. Someday we will be out of this land. We must not give up hope. The place where our children are born does not matter. What does matter is that we are alive. We are a family. We have each other. We are rebuilding." He holds me close. "Riva, our children are the future. We must live with hope for a bright future."

"Hope," I whisper softly. "We drew strength from hope when all was hopeless. Hope of finding family again, hope that the day of freedom would come. Hope helped us survive. Now hope that our children will have a bright tomorrow gives life meaning again. You are right, Moniek. Our children bring us joy no matter where they are born."

"If it is a boy"—Moniek's voice is low—"we'll name him Avrom, after your father. If it is a girl, Nacha, after your mother."

My eyes well up with tears. Names. That is all we have left. Names. No visible traces of their lives. No pictures to show our children. Only memories of faces that fade in and out.

How do I pass on the memories without falling apart each time the names are spoken? Will I ever have the strength to speak of them to my children? To share memories without tears?

I must not cry in front of my children. They must grow up in a normal world like other children. I must shelter them from our sorrow, from our pain. They must live normal lives. But can their world be normal however hard we try? Can I, can Moniek, can any survivor put a smile on his lips as his heart screams in agony? As his mind is filled with memories of horror? As faces of family float before him, calling, remember, remember?

"Children are the greatest treasure."

Moniek's voice sounds far away. "I remember my mother saying children are the greatest treasure. They make life worth living." His brown eyes filled with sadness, he stares at the window. He very, very seldom speaks of his family—mother, father, two brothers. Sometimes I try to draw him out. I would like to know them. They would have been my family now. His answers are always short, abrupt.

"Your mother was very wise, Moniek."

He does not answer.

"Were you close to your mother?"

Now a soft grin appears on his face. He turns toward me. "I was her best helper, she would say. 'I have no daughter, but you are more help than some daughters I know.' It made me feel proud, useful. She always worked so hard to make us a good home. I liked to help make her life a little easier." His voice breaks. He turns his face toward the window again.

"You had a good mother. You were a good son. You have happy memories. I am glad that you have happy memories. Your mother was right. Children are the greatest treasure."

"My mother was right," he repeats. "I wish I could keep her face in my mind. It keeps fading in and out. Only her eyes remain vivid, big, brown, soft."

"Big, brown, soft, like yours." I wipe the

tears from his eyes. "Big, brown, soft, and moist."

He smiles.

"You know, Moniek, you have a warm smile. If you would only smile more often."

"I smile when I have reason to smile."

"Well, what gives you reason to smile?"

His face is all bright now. "You. Laibele. The thought of a new baby on the way."

thirty-four

THE DISPLACED PERSONS camp in Leipheim is being liquidated. "Resettled to another place."

Resettled. The word brings back painful memories of August 1944. I see before me again the S.S. commandant of the ghetto of Lodz, Hans Biebow, a smile on his lips, relaxed. He speaks calmly, softly. *I am here today, ladies and gentlemen, because I am your friend. I care what happens to you. You are very, very important to us. We need your skilled labor. We need your talent. Listen to me, ladies and gentlemen, I personally urge you to report to the railroad station for resettlement to a different place of work.*

Trust me, ladies and gentlemen. Trust me, please. Not a hair will be harmed on anyone's head. Families will stay together. Trust me, please.

Do not trust anyone! Do not trust anyone! voices shout in my head. *We perished because we trusted. Do not trust anyone.*

I hear the same mistrust, the same fear in the voices of the other survivors in the camp.

"Why do they want to move us?"

"Where to?"

"They say they are combining camps. We've heard that before."

"They want to resettle us. We were 'resettled.' Death waited for us at the end of the trip."

"I never saw my children again," a woman wails.

"Let's not panic." Someone raises his voice to be heard above the others. "It is not the Germans who are going to resettle us. It is the UNRRA. We can trust them."

"We cannot trust anyone anymore," many voices call at once.

"Trust me, ladies and gentlemen. . . . Not a hair will be harmed on anyone's head."

"Do not trust anyone," I whisper.

A meeting is called. "My friends," someone says, "let's not panic. We must not panic. Some of us were fortunate. They got visas for permanent homes in other countries. We who remain in this camp must not give up hope. Someday some country will open its doors for us, too. We, too, will have a home. We, too, will live normal lives finally." He clears his throat. "But, meanwhile it has become necessary to combine some of the camps. It will be less of a burden. I suppose the organizations here did not expect us to be displaced for so long, either." He sighs. "They, too, wait as we do for the world to embrace those who escaped annihilation."

He clears his throat again. "The world was silent then, and the world remains silent. The world is so big, but for us there is no place. . . . I know how we all feel when we hear 'resettlement.' We are especially sensitive to certain words. But remember, friends, it is the Americans, not the Germans, who are doing the resettling. We are being sent to a displaced persons camp in Lechfeld. Let's not panic. It will not be done overnight. It will be orderly. Families will stay together."

Families will stay together. Trust me.

I look around me. This is not the ghetto factory where the S.S. commandant urged us warmly to stay together. But, still, it is Germany. Still, it is a former concentration camp. I stare at the speaker before us. He is not an S.S. commandant who has orders to send us to Auschwitz, to death. This man is a Holocaust survivor who lost his family. He is one of us. We must trust him.

"The camp administration is working on making the transfer smooth." His voice echoes in the stillness of the room. "The first to be transferred will be representatives of various committees who will get things organized. The last will be the camp police and their families."

My heart stops. We will not leave

together as a family. My brother-in-law Yosef is a member of the clothing committee. He, Mala, and their children, Abramek and Esther, must leave first. Moniek, Laibele, and I, Chana, Moishe, and Shiele will remain here to leave with the last group. Our husbands are in the camp police.

Tears well up in my eyes. We will be separated. We will have to say good-bye. Each time I said good-bye in the ghetto it was forever.

In 1942, as the wagon filled with Jewish men, women, and children sped off to the unknown, I shouted in horror to Mama, "Be strong." I never saw her again.

In 1943, I touched my brother Laibele's dead face with trembling hands as he was carried out of our home to be piled onto a wagon with other dead Jewish men, women, and children.

In 1944, I said good-bye to my brothers Motele and Moishele in a crowded cattle car, as we held on to one another. I still hear Motele's voice. *You must be strong. We must live. We must survive.* I never saw them again. I am afraid to say good-bye.

"Riva, it is only a short separation." Mala reads my thoughts. She holds me close to her. "We will be together soon. It is only a short separation." Tears flow down her cheeks. We hold each other tight.

thirty-five

MY HEART POUNDS as I stare at the letter before me. It is an official letter concerning our immigration to America. Moniek and I are requested to appear for an interview with an American official.

"The first step toward immigration." Moniek is overjoyed. "Our baby may be born in America yet."

I, too, am overjoyed, but I will be leaving my sisters in Germany. From one camp to another may be a short separation. From Germany to America may be a separation forever.

"We are going to America?" Laibele's eye are wide with wonder. "We are going to America, really?"

"If all goes well." My voice trembles. "If all goes well."

"Are we all going?"

"Daddy, you, and I may be getting visas." I try to smile.

"But what about the rest of the family? My aunts? My uncles? My cousins? They cannot come?" His voice is filled with fear. "Will they stay here forever?"

I feel a sharp stabbing pain in my chest. "Someday they, too, may get visas. But not yet."

His eyes are full of tears. "I do not want to leave without them."

"I do not want to leave without them, either, Laibele." I take him in my arms. "We have no choice."

He stares at me. "Why can't we stay here with them?"

"Because we do not want to remain in Germany forever. We must take advantage of the chance we are getting. We may not have another chance."

"Will I ever see them again?" The pain in his young voice breaks my heart.

"We must hope. We must hope, Laibele. Maybe when we get to America we can get visas for them."

"Can we really?" His face lights up.

"We must hope that we will be together again."

"We will, Mommy. We will." His cheerful voice fills the room. "We will. We will."

"From your mouth to God's ears," I whisper.

Moniek and I sit nervously in the waiting room of the American official. Others with letters in their hands seem just as restless. Our eyes are on the door of the official's office. Each time someone enters we wish him luck with trembling lips. We study the flushed faces of the ones who leave. Did they pass, or were they rejected? Our lives are in the hands of the stranger behind that closed door.

Finally our turn comes. My feet buckle as our names are called.

A man in his forties, his hair slightly gray at the temples, greets us cordially. His desk is covered with files. He points to the chairs in front of his desk. "Please, be seated."

He studies us carefully from behind his thick glasses. My heart pounds. Our destiny is in his hands. Slowly, carefully, he checks our names, birthdays, places of birth.

The presence of a government official fills me with fear. In Poland a government official always meant trouble. Our lives were threatened by government officials. A Jew in Poland never felt safe.

I look straight at the man before me. He is a government official. But this is not Poland. Still, he is a government official. "Why do you want to go to America?" His voice is inquisitive, challenging.

"I have family in Boston," Moniek replies. His voice betrays his nervousness.

"How will you support your wife and child?" His eyes are on Moniek's face.

"I will find a job as a carpenter," Moniek replies quickly. "I studied carpentry at the ORT school at the displaced persons camp."

"And if you cannot find work in this trade, what then?"

"I will work at anything I can. I will support my family." Moniek's voice is strong and confident.

The official looks slowly around the room, gazes through the window for a moment, then turns toward Moniek. "Are you a member of the Communist party?"

"No." Moniek looks straight at him.

"Were you ever a member?" He raises his voice.

"No, sir. I am not now and never have been a member of the Communist party."

"Were you ever a member of the Nazi party?" He sounds embarrassed.

We look at him, bewildered. He lowers his voice. "I must ask these questions. Were you ever a member of the Nazi party?"

Moniek pulls up his shirt sleeve. His eyes flash angrily. He puts his left arm on the desk. The number 75087, tattooed with blue ink across his arm, faces the official.

"Sir, I am a Jew. I spent five years of my life, my youth, in Auschwitz. My whole family perished, murdered by the Nazis." There is pain and outrage in his voice. He stares at the American official. "I am the only survivor of my family. The only survivor." His voice breaks. I take his hand quickly in mine.

"I am sorry." The official lowers his

eyes. "I am very sorry. I have to ask this question. Some Nazis pose as survivors to escape justice. It must have been hell."

Moniek swallows hard. "More than hell."

The gray eyes of the man behind the desk look at me softly. There is compassion in them. I feel more at east now.

"I must ask certain questions and write down your answers." He studies my face. Stares at the papers before him, then at me again. "Were you ever a prostitute?"

I gasp. My face burns from the insulting question. Tears fill my eyes. "No. No."

He lowers his eyes again. "Some questions are not pleasant. But they must be asked. Are you or were you a Communist?"

"No. No."

"Were you a Nazi?"

I feel like steel hands are clutching at my throat. I shake my head no.

"Sorry, you must answer."

"No." My voice sounds as if it is coming from a grave.

"I am not here to hurt you. God knows, you have been hurt enough."

He stands up and takes my hand in his. "You are very brave people. I do not know if I could survive all that." He presses my hand warmly. "You will build a new life. I wish you well."

He closes the files. "You still have to go

through medical examinations. You have a long road before you. You must not lose hope."

"As long as there is life, there is hope."

"As long as there is life, there is hope," he repeats. "I must remember that."

thirty-six

THE DISPLACED PERSONS camp in Leipheim is slowly being emptied. Soon our turn will come to be resettled again. Since 1946, we have passed through the camps in Berlin, München, Pocking, Leipheim, and now we are being sent to Lechfeld. Five camps in three years. Will our wandering ever end?

The long, painful journeys in cattle cars, trucks, from the ghetto to the death camp, from the death camp to the labor camp are forever with me. Each time we board a truck to be moved from one displaced persons camp to another, the horror of the past comes back to haunt me.

Hope and fear mingle. The hope that this is the last camp in Germany we may have to endure makes my heart beat faster. But the horrible fear, the fear that we may never leave Germany, that we may be doomed to wander from camp to camp, never live a normal life, makes me cry.

The world will embrace us when the gates of the death camps open. How often I heard those words spoken by the girls in the concentration camps. *The free world is waiting for us.*

It is now four years since liberation. We are still here. Do we live with false hope? Does the world care?

The interview with the American official sparked some hope. Still, there is a medical examination. That fills me with dread. Many of the survivors are refused visas to other countries because of health problems.

Tuberculosis spread easily in the ghettos, concentration camps, in hiding places. Malnutrition, overcrowding, horrible sanitary conditions, no medical care were the causes. The highly contagious disease hit everywhere. Many died. Those who survived and still carry traces of tuberculosis are now being punished by being rejected for immigration.

I see before me the pale face of my little brother, Laibele. He pleads with me, *Riva, I am very contagious. Do not hold me in your arms. Do not sit so close to me. Please, Riva.*

Don't you know I am in no danger of contracting tuberculosis? Don't you know that?

Why are you not in danger?

Well, you silly goose, you say I am a mother now. I remember hearing somewhere that God protects mothers from getting sick. Mothers have to be well to take care of their sick children. Well, if I am a mother I am safe.

I am tested for tuberculosis in the

displaced persons camp. The test is negative. Does God protect mothers?

Moniek, too, is tested. His result is positive. The UNRRA doctors offer to send him to a sanitorium in Germany for treatment. "I feel fine. I have no problem. I will not leave my wife and child alone," he argues.

"Conditions in the sanitorium are better than here, in the displaced persons camp," says the doctor. "Rest. Good food. Medical care. You will heal faster in a sanitorium."

"I will do everything you ask me to do, Doctor, but here. I will not leave my family."

Suddenly Moniek's voice fills with panic. "Doctor, am I endangering them?"

"You have traces of tuberculosis. But your family is safe."

"Thank you, Doctor."

The doctor shrugs his shoulders. "I understand," he murmurs.

He is under the doctor's care until told that he is all right. But what if they reject us because Moniek had tuberculosis at one time? Will our past keep the future in a free country away from us? Did we not suffer enough? I read the same troubled questions in Moniek's eyes. Still, we do not speak about them.

I look at the shining eyes of my little boy playing. I think of the new life growing within me. I must not lose hope. There must be a better tomorrow for them.

Laibele sits on the floor. His little fingers propel a paper boat back and forth. "Mommy," he says, "do people in America live in camps?"

His question startles me. He was born in a displaced persons camp. This is the only way of life he knows. Each new home is another camp.

I sit down next to him on the floor. He moves closer to me. "Do people in America live in camps? Will we live in another camp in America?" He continues to glide the paper boat over the floor, bouncing it softly up and down.

"No, my darling. In America people live in cities, towns, homes. Buildings big and small."

"No camps?"

"No camps. No camps."

His paper boat rests on the floor. He takes the boat in his hand again, pushes it slowly forward. "I will like living in America," he proclaims. "I will like living in America. Will we go there soon, Mommy?"

"I hope so, my love. I hope so."

thirty-seven

I SIT IN the truck that stands ready to transfer us to the displaced persons camp in Lechfeld. I hold my son on my lap. Moniek puts our bundles on the truck. I feel panic overtaking me. My head fills with voices—tormented, horror-filled voices. *Hold on to life! Be strong! Remember!*

The last good-byes, the agonizing outcries wail within me. I want to jump from the truck. I must be strong. I am free. This truck is not taking us to a concentration camp.

I press my child close to my heart. Hold him tight. The truck speeds forward.

Lechfeld, our new home. Again, long buildings covering a large area, resembling a concentration camp. Moniek stares at the camp before us silently. Dark, painful memories are written on his face.

The truck stops. My brother-in-law Yosef waits for us. I fall into his arms, sobbing.

"It is all right, Riva. I know it looks like a concentration camp. But there are family homes located on the other side of the camp. I managed to get housing there." He takes my hand, guides me forward. "There is a group of small homes with several three-room apartments. We put two families in each apartment so we could house all the new arrivals. Even to share an apartment will be nicer than to live in these buildings.

"I had to use my influence to get you and Chana into apartments. I could not get one apartment for the two families, but I got you all into the same house." He smiles. "I had to take what I could get. Chana will share an apartment with a family upstairs, and you will share an apartment with friends of mine from my hometown, Kalish, downstairs. They are nice people." He puts his arm around me. "At least you will be in the same house. Mala, our children, and I also live nearby."

I press close to him. "I am so happy we are all together again. If we could only remain together."

We walk silently to our new home, passing the long, gloomy buildings around us. In the distance a group of small homes glisten in the sunlight. I remember passing homes like that while being herded like animals to slave labor. Now I am to live in one of those homes. I do not feel any joy. We stop before one of the homes. The front door quickly opens. A smiling woman, her dark hair brushed to the side, runs toward us, followed by a man with his hand extended in greeting. "My name is Esther Kop and this is my husband, Moishe." Her voice is friendly and warm. "I feel that I know you already. Mala and Yosef talk about you often. Welcome. Welcome."

We follow her into the house. She takes us to the apartment we will share. A small entrance hall leads to two bedrooms, a kitchen, a bathroom. I remain standing in the entrance hall, wondering about the previous occupants: Who were they? Was there blood on their hands? Where are they now?

Esther takes me by the hand. "Come on. Don't just stand there. This is your home now." She pulls me gently into one of the rooms. It is large, sunny. "This is your room. Moishe and I have no children." There is a sadness in her voice that disappears quickly. "So we gave you the larger room. We are only two, and you are three, soon to be four. You need more room."

Moishe nods his head in agreement. "It will be nice to have a child here. I love children." He takes Laibele by the hand. "Come, I have a ball for you to play with."

"Let me show you the kitchen." Esther bounces from room to room. I follow her. The kitchen is comfortable, cheerful. White curtains move softly in the breeze coming through the open window. I feel strange in this place.

Esther studies my face quietly. "I know how you feel." She looks at the buildings in the distance. "Remember, we survived them." She puts her arms around me. "We are alive. I feel like you are my family."

"I feel the same way, Esther."

"Now you rest a little. You are an expectant mother. I will take care of dinner. You'll get organized later. Right now, rest."

My eyes fill with tears. I just met this woman and her husband, and already I feel at home with them, like a family reunited again. I stretch out on the bed, thinking of the Kops, their warmth, their gentleness, their caring. Each time I see these qualities in the survivors of horror, degradation, death, I am awed.

thirty-eight

"WE PASSED THE first test, the interview with the American official." Moniek holds a letter in his hands. His voice is tense. "Now, test two—the medical. Let's hope this, too, will go well."

"Let's hope. Let's hope."

We enter the German medical center for our physicals. The sound of German, the German doctors and nurses around me make me shiver. "They are not going to hurt us," Moniek whispers. "Calm down."

We are put into separate rooms. A nurse in a starched white uniform enters the room. "Undress, please," she says.

My hands shake as I try to unbutton my dress. Suddenly I am in Auschwitz again. The lines push forward. Harsh, loud commands. *Undress! Leave your clothes here! Move forward! Move!* I am naked, dazed. *Undress! Move forward! Left! Right!*

"Undress, please. We are not going to hurt you here." The nurse's voice, softer now, brings me back to the present. "Don't be afraid. We are not going to harm you."

Her face is close to mine. Her hair is pulled back under her nurse's cap. She is an elderly woman. There is compassion in her face. Pity in her voice. "Stop shaking, please. We will not hurt you." She turns and leaves the room.

The doctor enters. A man in his forties with thick glasses. He examines me carefully, asks a few questions, not looking directly at me. He sends me for X rays and tests.

Moniek rushes toward me as I finally return to the waiting room. "Are you all right? You look so pale, worn out."

I take his hand in mine. I feel safe. I rest my head on his shoulder.

"Our lives are still in their hands," he mumbles angrily.

The receptionist calls our names. "You may go home now," she informs us politely.

I take Moniek's arm. "Where is home?"

"Maybe soon in America. Maybe in America," he replies, a soft smile on his lips.

We await eagerly the results of the medical examinations. Restless, nervous, excited, we wait. The wait seems endless.

Finally an official letter from the immigration office. We stare at the letter, eager to open it but afraid of what news it may bring. With trembling hands I open the envelope. I read quickly.

Moniek passed the medical tests. I did not. I am requested to come back for more tests. I sit down heavily on the bed. My head spins. I was worried about Moniek's medical history. He had tuberculosis once. I did not think that I might fail the physical. I am pregnant, but this is not a disease. "What is wrong with me? Will my unborn child be affected?" I cry bitterly.

Moniek holds me tight. "Darling, it may not be anything serious. Calm down, please." He wipes the tears from my eyes. "Getting upset will not help. The baby will be fine. It may just take us a little longer to get out of here."

I take more tests. They cause a lot of discomfort and seem endless. The doctors ask many questions but do not give any answers to my questions.

"Did you have tuberculosis?"

"No."

"Were you exposed to tuberculosis?"

My brother Laibele's face floats before me. My heart beats fast. "Yes. What is wrong with me, Doctor?"

"I am not permitted to give out any information." A polite reply.

"Who then?"

"The Americans."

"Will I be able to go to America?" I persist.

"I am not permitted to answer any questions. Please do not ask me." The doctor is annoyed. The tests drag on and on.

Finally a written notice comes from the immigration office. My lungs are not clear. Immigration to America will not be possible at this time. After the baby is born, I may be tested again. For the time being, our visa to America must be postponed to a later date. I feel crushed.

"But I was tested before for tuberculosis. The tests were negative. What about the baby? What will happen to the baby if I do have tuberculosis?"

"Look at the positive side, Riva." Chana smiles. "We will still be together when the baby is born. We'll get to meet the new child in our family. When the baby is born, all will be well, you'll see. I remember Mama saying, 'Each child brings its own luck.' The new baby will bring luck. Maybe we all will find a country, a home." She sighs. "We keep on trying, and miracles do happen, right?"

"Yes, they do," I reply. "They do."

thirty-nine

JULY 7, 1949. My heart overflows with joy as I stare at the miracle in my arms, my newborn son. Moniek, his face radiant, holds my hand. "We have a healthy son, Riva. The doctor said he is fine."

I sigh a deep sigh of relief. The heavy burden, the constant fear that the baby will not be healthy has been lifted. "Thank heaven." I kiss the baby's tiny fingers.

"Avrom. Your name is Avrom," I whisper. "After my father, your grandfather." I cuddle him. "My little Avromele." My eyes overflow. "I have two sons. We have two sons."

Moniek grins. "You're right. *We. We* have two sons. Two healthy, beautiful sons."

"Riva, do you know what date it is?" Moniek asks suddenly.

"Yes. July 7, 1949. The day I gave birth to a healthy, normal child."

"And . . ." His eyes shine. "And . . ."

I look puzzled.

He smiles. "And July 7, 1945, we became husband and wife."

"Today is our fourth anniversary." I laugh and cry. "What a wonderful gift we both received today. What a wonderful day. What a wonderful anniversary."

He rushes out, returns shortly holding a can of pineapple juice and paper cups. He pours the juice into the cups. "Let's toast our new baby and our fourth anniversary. We are very lucky, my love. We have each other. We have two healthy children."

I lift the cup joyfully. "*L'chaim*, darling. To life."

We touch cups. "To life. *L'chaim.*"

I am still in Germany. I am still in a displaced persons camp. But I feel at ease, calm, happy. A healthy child in my arms. A healthy child waiting for me in our room. Two sisters to share my happiness nearby.

I remember how alone we were when Laibele was born. Now we have a family. We are not alone anymore. Even the gloom of the bare room used as a camp hospital cannot dampen my spirit. We have a family. Laibele has a brother. Life is wonderful.

When we return to our apartment, Laibele stands in front of the house clenching a bunch of wildflowers. "Mommy! Mommy!" He runs toward us. He stops, stares at the baby in Moniek's arms. "He is so little." There is a trace of disappointment in his voice. "I thought he would be bigger."

He remembers the flowers in his hands.

"These are for you, Mommy. Esther helped me pick them in the field." His voice is full of pride. His shining eyes move quickly from me to the baby. He touches the baby's hand lightly. "I am your big brother, Laibele." He speaks softly. "Don't worry, Mommy. I will be careful with him, Mommy."

"I am sure you will be. Not so long ago, you, too, were very little, and look at you now. My big boy."

He smiles proudly, takes my hand, and leads me into the house.

I place the baby on the bed. "Laibele, do you want to help me change the baby's diaper?"

"Yes, Mommy, I'll help." He smiles as he hands me a diaper. "I am a big brother and a big helper."

Chana and Mala look on, smiling. Chana takes the baby in her arms, kissing his head. "I am happy that I get a chance to hold the baby in my arms. You see, Riva, whatever happens, some good comes of it. You could not leave, so we get a chance to enjoy the baby."

Mala's eyes fill with tears. "If only we could stay together." I feel the stabbing pain of reality. The uncertainty of our future creeps in even in moments of joy.

forty

I UNDERGO MEDICAL tests again and again. My lungs are not clear. Our immigration to America is postponed once more. We must wait to see if there are any changes in my lungs. I am beginning to lose hope of ever leaving Germany.

Yankl's wife, Edzia, has given birth in Canada to a second daughter, Faygele. He is trying to get visas for Chana, Moishe, and Shiele to bring them to Canada. HIAS is working on getting visas for Mala, Yosef, Abramek, and Esther. I hope the efforts on their behalf are successful. I remember Mama's words when her older children left for Russia: *Better in a faraway land, as long as they are alive.*

The medical tests are endless. We live from day to day. I draw strength from my children. Laibele is over three years old. Avromele, five months. They are both healthy.

Finally the news we were waiting for, hoping for: We will be permitted to go to America. My lungs do not show any changes. My condition is not contagious. The X rays will be given to me to take to America, as I must have a follow-up. And because we have a baby under six months, we will be sent by plane as soon as there is a place.

We read the letter again and again. Is it real? Could something go wrong? Could they change their minds? Could they find a reason to reject me again? My head spins.

"Moniek, do you think they will find a place on a plane before the baby is six months old? The journey by plane is shorter, more comfortable."

"Plane or ship, Riva, whatever, as long as we get to America." Moniek beams. "After all the years of waiting, dreaming, soon it will be a reality. Soon, soon we will go to America."

"And soon we will have to say good-bye." I gaze at my sisters.

The gloom of departure dampens our joy. Even the children are subdued.

Mala sits down on the bed, pulls me close. "Riva, we will always be together, no matter how far the distance that separates us." She removes a gold ring from her hand and slips it on my finger. "Each time you look at this ring, you will think of me." Her voice is low. "This ring was given to me by a fellow refugee. She had managed to hold on to some of the jewelry she had brought from

Poland. When we left Russia, we were allowed to bring out only what we had on. What she couldn't wear she gave to Chana and me to carry past inspections. The ring was her thank-you. This ring, too, journeyed from Poland to Russia to Germany, and now it will go to America. Riva, each time you look at the ring, remember, you are not alone."

I fight back my tears. Mala holds me tight.

"We will always be in one another's hearts," Chana says, "no matter how far apart."

"We must hope that we will be together again one day," I whisper.

forty-one

WE HAVE ORDERS to leave for Bremen, the port of departure by ship. We are assured that if there is a place on a plane soon, we will fly out from Bremen. There are still several weeks until the baby is six months old.

"Plane, ship, whatever—as long as we go to America." Laibele repeats the now-familiar words.

He sits on Moniek's lap. "Daddy, what will America be like?"

"For us, Laibele, it will be home."

"Home, home, home." He bounces on Moniek's knee, singing, "Home, home, home."

Bremen is crowded with refugees from many countries, all waiting for ships to take them "home." We are assigned sleeping areas, women and children in one huge hall, men in another. I feel alone as I stare at the cot and baby crib that will be our home until we depart. Surrounded by many, many strangers, I feel little and insignificant. I see in their faces, in their eyes, the same fears, the same pain, the same loneliness that I feel.

Laibele sits on the cot near me. Suddenly he puts his little arms around me. "I will take care of you and my brother when Daddy is not here, Mommy. Don't worry."

I take him into my arms. "I am so lucky to have you, my darling."

The huge room filled with cots, each cot someone's home, the turmoil, the sound of many, many voices remind me of ghettos, concentration camps. I see faces of loved ones, faces of friends, faces of strangers all hoping for tomorrow. All waiting to be free.

"I am free. I am alive. We will endure," I whisper.

Moniek takes the baby in his arms. "We survived much worse. We will not be here very long."

A woman in her late twenties rests on the cot next to mine. She nurses a baby. She turns toward us. She looks at us, her new neighbors, with pity and sadness. "Forgive me, but I think you should be prepared for a long stay here. I am here for more than a month already." Her voice is low. "There are more people here waiting for transport ships than there are ships. We must make the best of our stay." Her fingers move softly over the baby's face. "They will have a better life."

"They must have a better life." I, too, speak softly.

Moniek pulls our bundles from under

the cot. Holding a white sheet in his hands, he studies our surroundings like an architect about to design a home. "If this is going to be your home—at least for a while—I must find a way to give you some privacy." He rushes off.

Holding four dried branches, he returns sometime later. Silently he attaches the branches to the four corners of the cot, ties the sheet around the cot, forming a small hut. He smiles triumphantly. "Well, how do you like your new home, sweetheart?"

I smile, amused and proud. "That is very clever. You built us a fine home, darling."

He takes my hand in his. "In America we will have a better home."

"All this shall pass. I wish you could stay with us, but rules are rules. You must go now, Moniek. We will be all right."

"That's my girl." He hugs me tight. He takes Laibele in his arms and lifts him high into the air.

"You are in charge until I come back, my son."

"Don't worry, Daddy. I am a big boy," Laibele proclaims loud and clear.

I lie on the cot. Laibele is next to me, playing with his paper boat. The baby is fast asleep in the carriage. I remember Mala and Yosef bringing that carriage for Laibele all the way from Berlin to the displaced persons camp in Leipheim. How time flies. Now

Laibele is a "big boy," in charge of his mother and little brother.

The privacy curtain Moniek constructed keeps away the faces of the others but not their voices.

"Until you are on the ship, you are not yet on your way."

"Even from America, they can still send you back."

"Someone was just sent back to the displaced persons camp because of medical problems."

Medical problems. My heart beats faster. Medical problems. They can still send us back to the camp.

I move the sheet aside and turn to the woman on the next cot. "Do we still have to undergo medical tests here?" I ask.

"Some people are called for tests, some for shots, some for questions." She sighs. "It never ends."

Laibele's eyes are on my face. "It will be all right, Mommy. We will go to America."

forty-two

A MONTH HAS already passed since we arrived in Bremen. More tests, more shots, more questions. The baby is over six months old. We cannot go by plane. We are waiting for a ship.

"Ship or plane, as long as we get there . . ."

Each time a transport leaves, our eyes gaze longingly at the ship. When will our turn come? Will it be soon?

People come and go. I am afraid to get close to anyone. It hurts to say good-bye. My little family is my whole world. If only we could leave soon.

"We are leaving! We are leaving!" Moniek runs across the huge hall, shouting. "We are scheduled for the U.S.A.T. *General A.W. Greely*. It is to leave soon." He whirls me around joyfully. "Our turn has come."

I hug him happily.

The U.S.A.T. *General A.W. Greely* is a military transport ship used to bring survivors of the Holocaust to the land of their dreams, America. Many, many people wait at the shore. "There are so many people here. Is there enough room for all?" I ask Moniek.

"Many people are here just to watch the ship leave. Calm down."

A woman cuddling a baby moves close to me. "Are you leaving on this ship?"

"I hope so. I hope so," I reply slowly.

"Could you—would you—" she stammers. "Would you leave your carriage for my baby? You are going to America. I will still remain here for a long time." Her eyes plead gently. "It is for my baby's sake that I swallow my pride. Would you—"

I gaze at her forlorn face, look at her thin arms that must ache from carrying the baby. I take Avromele out of the carriage. "Here, dear woman. May your baby use it in good health. In America we will have another carriage."

"May God bless you with health, happiness, and a safe journey." She puts the baby quickly into the carriage. "Have a safe journey and good luck." She smiles happily.

"Have a safe journey! Have a safe journey!" others call as they wave to us. I know what they feel. I know what they are thinking. I wish them, too, a safe journey very soon.

We are called. I am on the ship and still wondering if it is real. Are we on a ship to America, to a new land, a home?

We are taken to the lower level, where

the men are separated from the women and children. The cabin I enter has some bunk beds and a baby crib. I put the baby into the crib and settle Laibele on the bunk we will share. The cabin is small and cramped, but nothing could take away from the joy of this moment. We are finally leaving. It has been five years. Five years since our liberation from concentration camps. Now we will know what freedom is. We are leaving Germany. We are really free.

"Mommy, when can I see the whole ship? It is so big." Laibele is filled with the excitement of finally being on a real ship. Finally going to America.

"As soon as Daddy comes."

"Can I see the captain? I'd like to see a real captain."

"I am sure the captain is too busy. He has a lot of important duties to take care of. He has to guide this ship to America."

"I wish I could see the captain."

"Calm down, my love. Calm down." I take his hand.

Three other women settle on the other bunks. "My little boy was too old for the cabin. He has to stay with the men below," one says. "I hope he will be all right."

"I am sure he will be all right. He is with his father," replies another. "You are lucky to have children," she adds softly.

I look at the women I will share this very special journey with. It is hard to tell their ages. They seem young and old at the same time. The same sorrow, the same pain lingers in their eyes. Do I look like that, I wonder.

Moniek enters, smiling. "You ladies have a real palace. You should see the crowded place I am in. But who cares? We are going to America." He hugs us happily. "I volunteered to do some work on the ship, help in the kitchen, paint the ship. I want to be useful."

"Can I help paint the ship, Daddy?" Laibele asks eagerly.

"I think you're a little too young, my son."

Laibele's face clouds with disappointment.

"You have an important job right here, Laibele. You have to take care of your mommy and little brother," Moniek adds.

"I will do a good job, Daddy." He is all smiles again.

Moniek takes Laibele's hand. "Now let's check out the boat."

I take the baby in my arms. My joy is mixed with apprehension. It is January. Will we encounter storms on the ocean? Will we arrive safely in America? What if they do not let us in? What if they find a reason to send us back?

The woman on the bunk across from mine stares at me as I nurse the baby. She turns away, hiding her face in the pillow. I hear her sob. I watch her silently. We have learned not to ask too many questions of one another.

She wipes her eyes and looks at me again. "Forgive me. I try to control myself, but when I see a mother with children I break down." She stares at the porthole. "It is such a big world out there. But my world will always be empty without my children." She turns toward me. "They took them from me, my two little girls. Tore them from me. I never saw them again. I still go on living, if this is living. . . . I lost them all, my husband, my children, my family. Why did God spare me? Why did God let me live? I would be better off dead. Why did I survive?"

Her pain-filled questions cut deep into my heart. How many times do I, do others ask, why did I survive?

I wipe the tears from my face. "There must be a reason why we survived, why we go on living."

She stares at me silently.

"We are alive to speak for our dead, to remember them, to rebuild."

"You found strength surrounded by horror, death—"

She raises her voice. "But I had hope

then that I would find them alive. Now there is only emptiness."

"You will find the strength," I tell her. "You are alive. You will live."

forty-three

WE ASSEMBLE IN a huge dining room for our first meal on the boat. Many tables are laden with bread, butter, cheeses, sausages, and strange-looking paper cartons fill the hall. The hungry passengers gather at the tables. Some fill their plates eagerly. Others stare confused at the cartons.

"What do you think is in the paper cartons?" a woman near me asks.

I read the letters on the carton. It says milk. How can there be milk in a paper container? I wonder.

"Milk and meat!" the woman shouts. "How can a Jew eat milk and meat at the same time! It is forbidden!"

"But, dear lady, not all of us are Jews, and not all who are Jews are observant," a man calls from across the table, his mouth filled with food.

The woman lowers her eyes. "I am sorry. Eat in good health. I am not very observant. Still, there was never milk and meat on the same table in my home."

"Your home is no more," someone calls

bitterly. "What was, is no more. Eat and be grateful for the food."

She turns toward me. "I cannot eat milk and meat. I cannot."

"I know how you feel. But eat the bread and milk, or you will go back to your bunk hungry."

She nibbles at the bread, guilt written on her pained face.

"I never saw milk in a paper box, Mommy." Laibele stares at the carton. "You always boiled the milk that you bought, and then we drank it. Did they boil the milk already? Why is the milk in a paper box, not in a pot?"

I, too, wonder. "I am sure no one here has seen milk in a carton before, Laibele. I hope it is safe to drink. This is the first of many new, strange customs we will learn in the new land. Many new and strange customs, Laibele."

I pour a little milk in a cup, taste it. "It tastes all right. I am sure they would not give us anything that would make us ill."

"Can I drink some, Mommy?"

I hesitate for a moment. "Well, just a little bit. You are not used to milk that comes from a paper carton."

He sips slowly. A smile covers his face. "I just learned a new custom. I drink milk like an American."

Moniek grins. "It won't take him long to become an America."

The ship moves forward, rocking back and forth. The happy, eager passengers become seasick. They vomit, curl up in pain from motion sickness.

Moniek is fine, busy painting the boat. The seasickness somehow does not affect him. Laibele and the baby, too, are well. I stay on my bunk, too sick to move, too weak to nurse the baby.

My heart breaks as I hear the baby cry. Poor child is hungry, but I cannot hold down any food. I have nothing to nurse him with. I crawl into the baby's crib to comfort him with my nearness. He stops crying for a while, then begins again.

Laibele, his eyes full of fear, caresses my hand softly. "Mommy, Mommy, please don't be sick, please."

I press his hand weakly.

Moniek brings a nurse to see me. She takes the baby into her arms. "Poor child. You are starved. We will give you a bottle of milk."

I raise my head. "My baby never had bottled milk. Could he get sick from it?"

"My dear woman, you have no food to give him. Your baby will get sick without food."

"But he never had milk from a bottle."

"There is a first time for everything. He needs nutrition." She puts the baby in Moniek's arms and leaves.

She returns shortly with a baby bottle in her hands. "Don't look so sad," she says to me as she takes the baby in her arms again. "It is not a crime to give a baby milk from a bottle." She puts the nipple of the bottle into the baby's mouth. The baby drinks the milk hungrily.

"Look, look how well Avromele drinks the milk from a bottle, Mommy," Laibele calls. "I drink milk from a carton. He drinks milk from a bottle. We are both new Americans."

I smile weak, still feeling guilty.

Moniek returns to his work. I remain in the crib near the baby. Laibele sits on the bunk, keeping his eyes on us. "Go to sleep, Mommy. I will watch over my brother. You sleep."

I am too sick to argue. My eyes close heavily.

Moniek returns later in the evening. "I have an orange for you, Riva. This will make you feel better." He slips a piece of the juicy orange into my mouth. "Bite into it, Riva. Come on, bite into it."

Suddenly I am back in the ghetto again. My little brother Moishele slips something into my mouth as I lie in bed swollen from malnutrition. *Bite into it. Bite into it,* he pleads.

I bite into the plump, soft object in my mouth. A burst of sweet, tangy juice fills my mouth with a long-forgotten taste. A tangerine. A real tangerine . . . in the ghetto?

We traded our ration of bread for it on the black market. It will help you get well. You'll see. You'll see.

My darling little brothers. They sold their bread. They went hungry for a whole week. They awaited a miracle from the tangerine.

Riva, you must get well, I hear them whisper.

"Bite into it, Riva. You must eat. You must get well." I hear Moniek's worried voice.

I open my eyes. "I will be fine."

The days pass slowly. Several storms rock the boat violently.

"Will we ever reach shore alive?"

"Did we survive only to die at sea?" My neighbors moan.

Moniek brings oranges for all. "Eat, girls. Keep up your strength. We will survive."

A week passes.

"Soon we will be in America." Moniek keeps up his pep talk. "Soon we will be in our new home."

The sea is getting calmer. I begin to feel better. People move about the boat now.

The electricity, the tension of the nearness of our long-awaited destination fills the air.

"We are approaching the New York harbor!" someone shouts.

The boat rocks gently now. The days of misery, seasickness are suddenly forgotten. The ship is filled with cries of joy. "America! America!"

"Look, Laibele, the Statue of Liberty is welcoming us to America. A home at last."

Six years of the ghetto, the death camp, the labor camps. Five years of wandering homeless through displaced persons camps. A home at last.

forty-four

FEBRUARY 2, 1950. We reach the shores of America, not knowing if we will ever again see my sisters, Mala and Chana, or my brother Yankl.

But then, by some miracle, Mala, Yosef, and their children get visas for America. Chana, Moishe, and their son get visas to be with Yankl. In 1955 they all come to America. Moniek never finds anyone in his immediate family.

Today I take stock of our family. Laibele (Louis) and Avromele (Allen) were both born in displaced persons camps in Germany. Our third son was born in the land of the free, October 30, 1950. We named him after Moniek's mother, Chava. *Chava* means "life." We used the masculine form, Chaim (Harvey). September 17, 1966, our daughter Nachele (Nancy) was born. My mother's name was passed on to my child.

Mala's son, Abram, was born in Siberia, her daughter, Eesther, in a displaced persons camp in Germany.

Chana's first son, Shiele (Stanley), was born in a displaced persons camp in Germany, her daughter Sore Nache (Susan) in Canada, her second son, Motel Baruch (Mark), in America.

Yankl's first daughter, Nacha (Nelsa), was born in a displaced persons camp in Germany, his two other daughters, Faygele (Fay) and Mashe (Marsha), in Canada.

In spite of everything, our family tree blossoms.

I still search for Motele and Moishele, for members of my family. I still write letters to various organization engaged in tracing lost families. Sometimes I study the faces of strangers or stop short when someone's voice sounds familiar.

As long as there is life, there is hope.